Uncle John's BATHROOM PUZZLER

SCRAMBLED

125 BRAND-NEW ANAGRAM PUZZLES

WORDS

PORTABLE
PRESS

Bathroom Readers' Institute
Ashland, Oregon, and San Diego, California

UNCLE JOHN'S BATHROOM PUZZLER
SCRAMBLED WORDS

"Bathroom Reader," "Portable Press," and
"Bathroom Readers' Institute" are registered trademarks
of Baker & Taylor, Inc. All rights reserved.

For information, write...
The Bathroom Readers' Institute
P.O. Box 1117, Ashland, OR 97520
www.bathroomreader.com / E-mail: mail@bathroomreader.com

ISBN-13: 978-1-60710-782-8 / ISBN-10: 1-60710-782-1

Printed in the United States of America
First printing: May 2013
1 2 3 4 5   17 16 15 14 13

FSC
www.fsc.org
MIX
Paper from
responsible sources
FSC® C101537

INTRODUCTION

Uncle John has spent the last few months locked in his office muttering to himself, but it wasn't until recently that he emerged to share what he'd been doing. All this time, everyone's favorite puzzle meister has been SCRAMBLING WORDS! Just so that he could proudly present the latest in his series of puzzle books.

Starting with the idea behind the parlor game Categories (or Scattergories for those who prefer board games), Uncle John and his team developed a twist on the old standard. They took groups of three letters and three categories and came up with their own answers...that are for us to know and you to find out!

HOW IT WORKS

• On each left-hand page you'll see a group of letters inside circles.
• On the right-hand page is a 3 x 3 grid made up of squares. The three letters across the top of the grid are the first letters of the word that each answer will start with.
• Down the left side of the grid, you'll find three categories.

The challenge is this: Unscramble the letters in the circles to make words that begin with each letter across the top of the grid. Then fit those words into the categories. The task may be as simple as puzzling out U.S. states or classic TV shows. Or it might be harder: natural disasters and bicycle parts. Given the letter Z and the category "Striped Animals," for example, you'd probably look for a set of scrambled letters A B E R Z, which would spell the word ZEBRA. And that's an easy one.

MIX IT UP

Also, as usual, we've added a few variations to make the puzzles more tricky:
• **Section 1** includes basic puzzles: nine squares and nine circles.
• **Section 2** adds this twist: There are nine squares and ten circles. One of those cicles is a red herring and includes a scrambled word that won't fit in the grid.
• **Section 3** looks pretty easy—there are nine squares and nine circles. But on

THANK YOU!

The Bathroom Readers' Institute sincerely thanks the following people whose advice, assistance, and hard work made this book possible.

Gordon Javna

JoAnn Padgett

Melinda Allman

Stephanie Spadaccini

Lidija Tomas

Patrick Merrell

Derek Fairbridge

Jay Newman

Monica Maestas

Aaron Guzman

Ginger Winters

Jennifer Frederick

Annie Lam

Lilian Nordland

Sydney Stanley

Trina Janssen

Brian Boone

Kim Griswell

Alfred Einstein

Felix the Wonder Dog

Sophie and JJ

Thomas Crapper

closer inspection, you'll see that the name of one of the categories is missing. You'll need to unscramble all the letters in all the circles to find out which three objects fit the missing category...and then figure out what that category is.

• **Section 4** also has nine squares and nine circles, but in one of those circles, we've substituted an illustration to stand in for the scrambled letters of a word. It's your job to figure out what that object is, unscramble the letters of its name, and put that word in the correct square.

If that sounds like a lot to remember, don't worry. We'll remind you of the directions on each page. So grab a pencil and start unscrambling! We wish you luck in your latest puzzling adventure!

As always, go with the flow...

—Uncle John and the BRI Staff

BASIC SCRAMBLES

Your job in this section is simple: Check out the three categories listed on the right-hand page and the letters that run across the top of the 3 x 3 answer grid. Then see if you can find—from among the circled letters on the left-hand page—a word that begins with each given letter and that fits the category. Write that word in the corresponding square.

PUZZLE 001

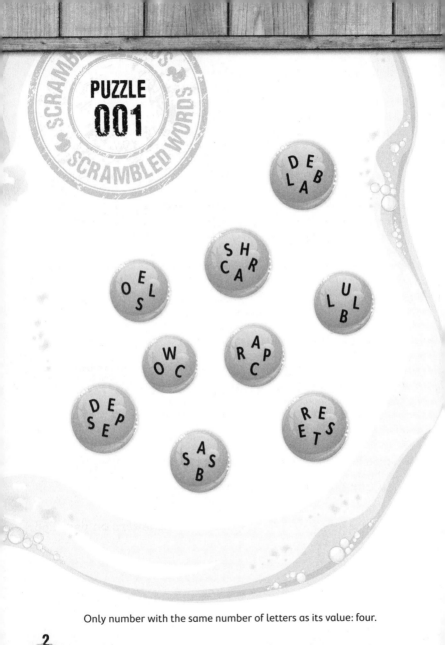

Only number with the same number of letters as its value: four.

	C	**B**	**S**
Cattle			
Movie titles			
Fish			

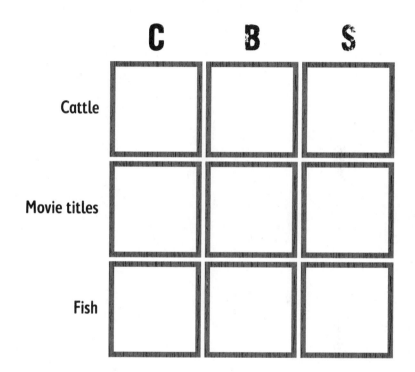

Answers on page 258.

Raw termites taste like pineapple.

3

In Canada, Canadian bacon is called "back bacon."

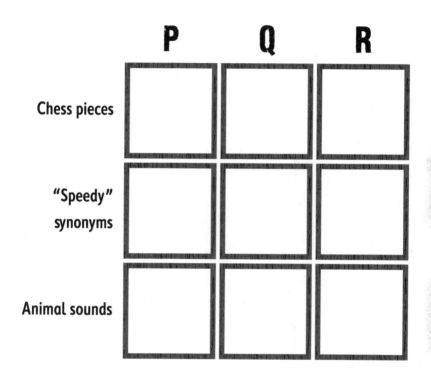

	P	**Q**	**R**
Chess pieces			
"Speedy" synonyms			
Animal sounds			

Answers on page 258.

U.S. president Grover Cleveland's first name was actualy Stephen.

Muppeteer Frank Oz described the character of Miss Piggy as…

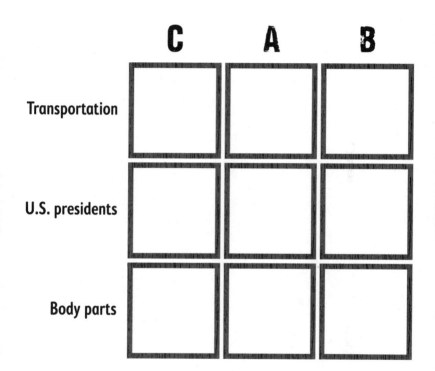

	C	**A**	**B**
Transportation			
U.S. presidents			
Body parts			

Answers on page 258.

..."a truck driver wanting to be a woman."

PUZZLE
004

Chad and Barbie Soper of Rockford, MI, had children on 8/8/08, 9/9/09, and 10/10/10.

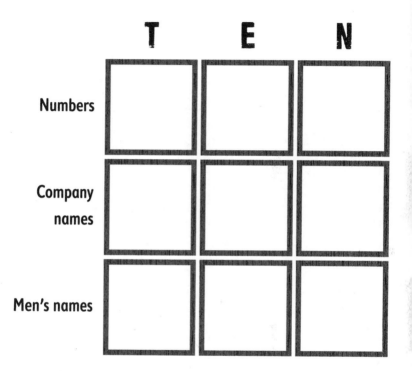

	T	**E**	**N**
Numbers			
Company names			
Men's names			

Answers on page 258.

In Turkey, the birds we call turkeys are known as *hindi*.

PUZZLE
005

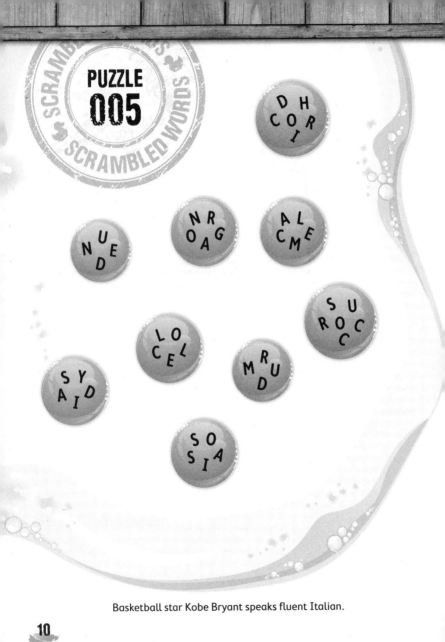

Basketball star Kobe Bryant speaks fluent Italian.

D O C

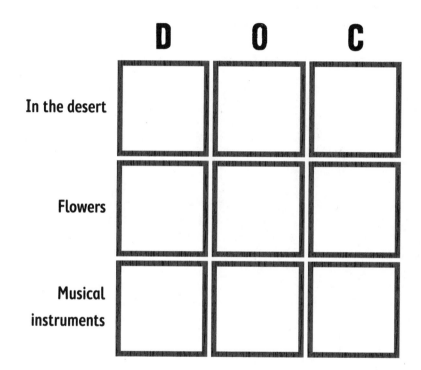

	D	O	C
In the desert			
Flowers			
Musical instruments			

Answers on page 258.

The average dog is as smart as a two-year-old child.

The origin of embarrassing dads? Ancient Romans wore socks with sandals.

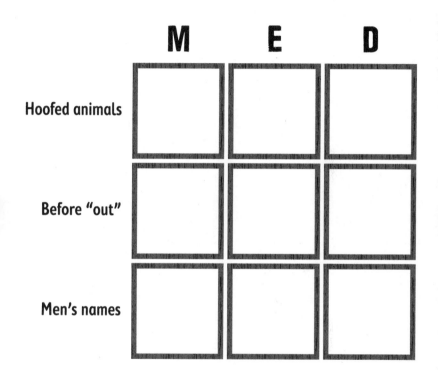

	M	**E**	**D**
Hoofed animals			
Before "out"			
Men's names			

Answers on page 259.

Number of words spoken by Arnold Schwarzenegger in *The Terminator*: 74.

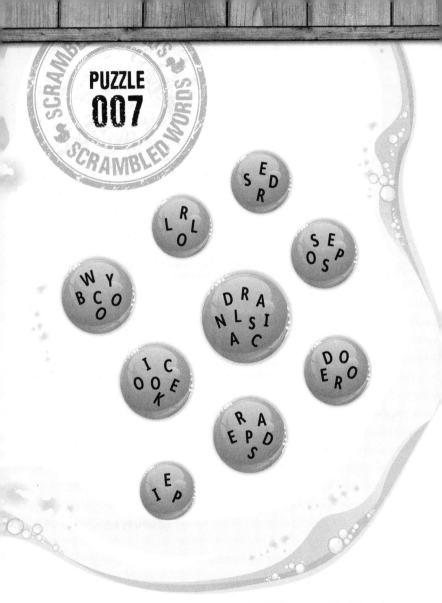

The first McDonald's drive-thru was created in 1975 near an AZ military base...

	C	**P**	**R**
Bakery items			
Baseball teams			
The Old West			

Answers on page 259.

...to serve soldiers who weren't allowed to get out of their cars wearing fatigues.

PUZZLE
008

It is illegal to enter the British House of Parliament in a suit of armor.

	P	**C**	**S**
Soda brands			
Sports			
After "down"			

Answers on page 259.

Actor Kevin Spacey's brother Randy makes his living as a Rod Stewart impersonator.

PUZZLE
009

Viagra and Rogaine were originally developed to treat high blood pressure.

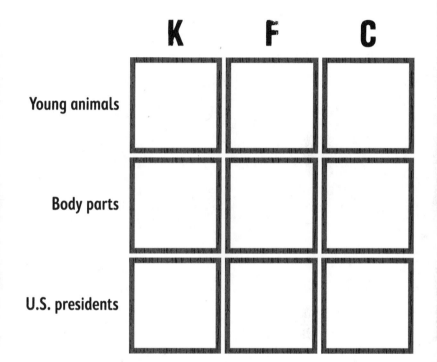

	K	**F**	**C**
Young animals			
Body parts			
U.S. presidents			

Answers on page 259.

The small pink nodule in the corner of your eye is called a *caruncula*.

PUZZLE 010

A L E
A C E
R

S U
B R H

N E C L
P L
I

L I
O L C
E

D E
L O P
O

O A N
C B

O N Y
O C A
R

G L
B A E
E

E N
A A K
P C

Q: Whose movie career began with *Citizen Kane* and ended with *Taxi Driver*?...

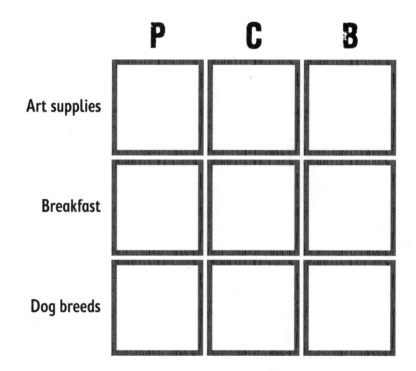

	P	C	B
Art supplies			
Breakfast			
Dog breeds			

Answers on page 259.

...A: Composer Bernard Hermann.

The giraffe has seven neck vertebrae—the same number as humans.

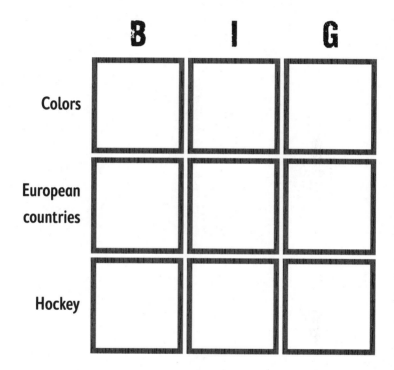

	B	I	G
Colors			
European countries			
Hockey			

Answers on page 260.

Only U.S. state that borders three different Canadian provinces: Montana.

A P
N E L

N O
A B C
R

A H
N I C

D I
I A N

O N N
E

A H D
O I

D R O
L O O
C A

A D A
A V N
E

O N I
D I E

There is a mushroom named for SpongeBob SquarePants.

	I	**N**	**C**
Asian countries			
Chemical elements			
U.S. states			

Answers on page 260.

Blue eyes are the result of a genetic mutation.

Napoleon wasn't actually short; he was 5'7"—average height for his era.

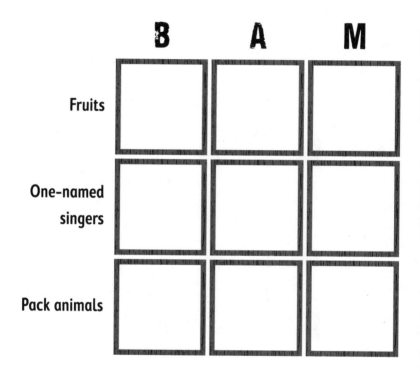

	B	**A**	**M**
Fruits			
One-named singers			
Pack animals			

Answers on page 260.

Spider silk has been used to make violin strings.

PUZZLE 014

Jamie Farr (aka Corporal Klinger) is the only M*A*S*H actor who has...

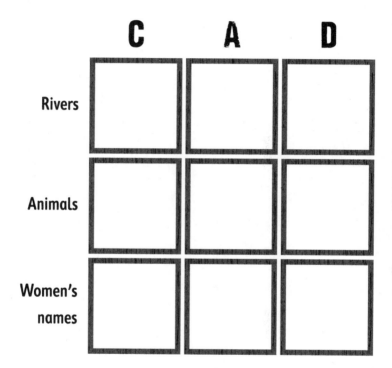

	C	**A**	**D**
Rivers			
Animals			
Women's names			

Answers on page 260.

...the same hometown (Toledo, Ohio) as his character.

Well, isn't that ironic? Caffeine acts as a pesticide for coffee plants.

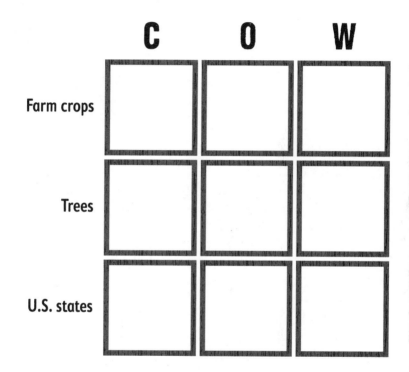

	C	O	W
Farm crops			
Trees			
U.S. states			

Answers on page 260.

George Washington preferred bowing to shaking hands.

PUZZLE 016

SCRAMBLED WORDS

President John F. Kennedy was a fan of James Bond novels.

	G	**E**	**M**
Broadway musicals			
After "after"			
Birds			

Answers on page 261.

Despite having six legs, dragonflies can't walk.

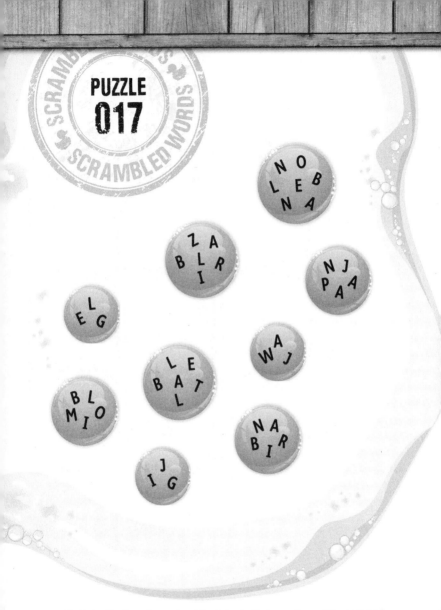

Technically, Americans should celebrate Independence Day on July 2...

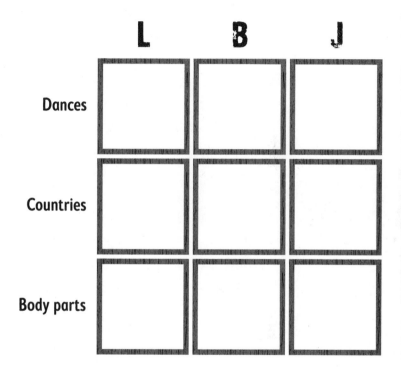

	L	**B**	**J**
Dances			
Countries			
Body parts			

Answers on page 261.

...That's when the new country declared itself free from Great Britain.

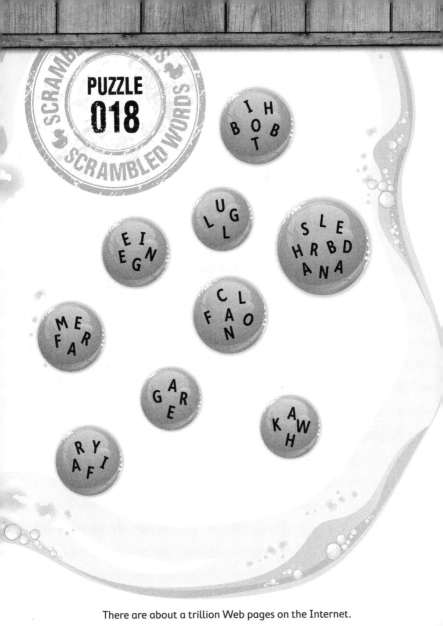

PUZZLE 018

I H
B O B
T

L U G
L

E I
E G N

S L E
H R B D
A N A

C L
F A O
N

M E
F A R

G A R
E

K A W
H

R Y I
A F

There are about a trillion Web pages on the Internet.

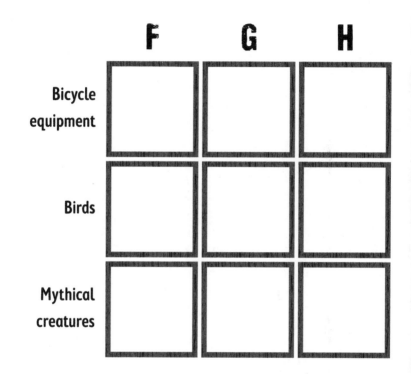

	F	**G**	**H**
Bicycle equipment			
Birds			
Mythical creatures			

Answers on page 261.

The city of Venice is not only sinking; it's also tilting eastward.

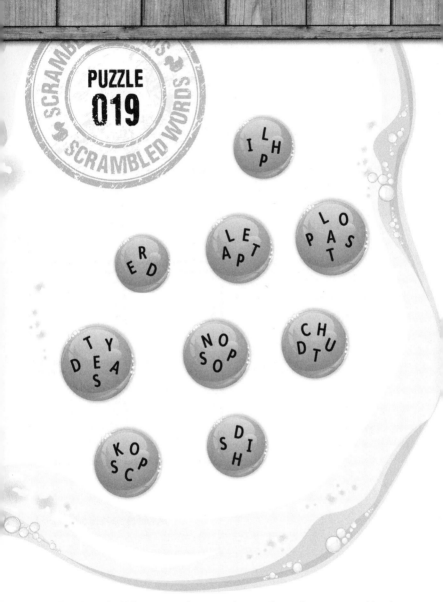

PUZZLE
019

People in the U.S. eat more bananas than apples and oranges combined.

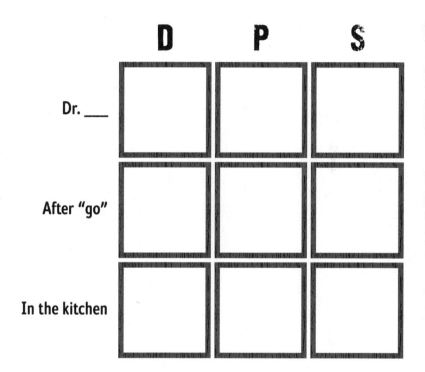

	D	**P**	**S**
Dr. ___			
After "go"			
In the kitchen			

Answers on page 261.

In the 1850s, Route 66 west of Albuquerque, NM, was a camel trail.

PUZZLE
020

The definition of horsepower: "The power required to lift 33,000 lbs by 1 foot...

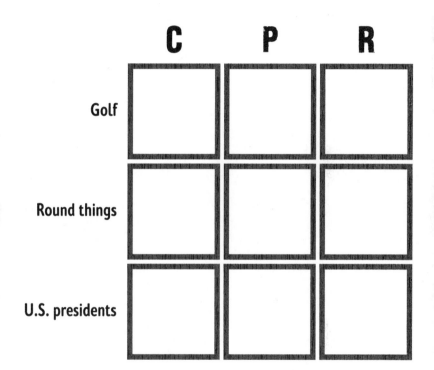

	C	**P**	**R**
Golf			
Round things			
U.S. presidents			

Answers on page 261.

…in 1 minute." That means a real horse has only 0.7 horsepower.

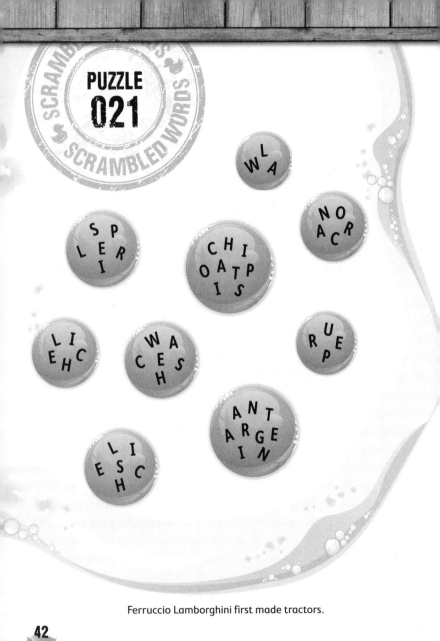

SCRAMBLED WORDS
SCRAMBLED WORDS

W L A

N O A C R

S P L E R I

C H I O A T P I S

L I E H C

W A C E S H

R U E P

L I E S C H

A N T A R G E I N

Ferruccio Lamborghini first made tractors.

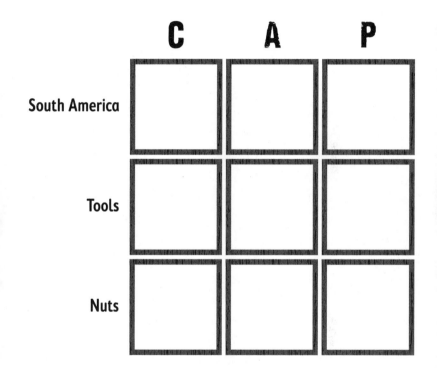

	C	**A**	**P**
South America			
Tools			
Nuts			

Answers on page 262.

The 100 tallest mountains on earth are all located in Asia.

SCRAMBLED WORDS

SI
R B
E E

F L
F A E
W

TW
H E

Z L
T W A

K R
E B A

N T
A

N T
G O A

T
E A

W O
B R N

The 1900 Olympics featured live pigeon shooting as an event...

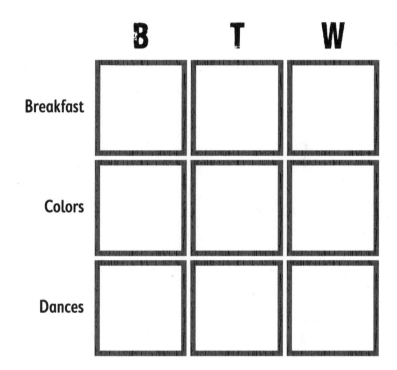

	B	**T**	**W**
Breakfast			
Colors			
Dances			

Answers on page 262.

…Belgium's Leon de London bagged 21 pigeons and won gold.

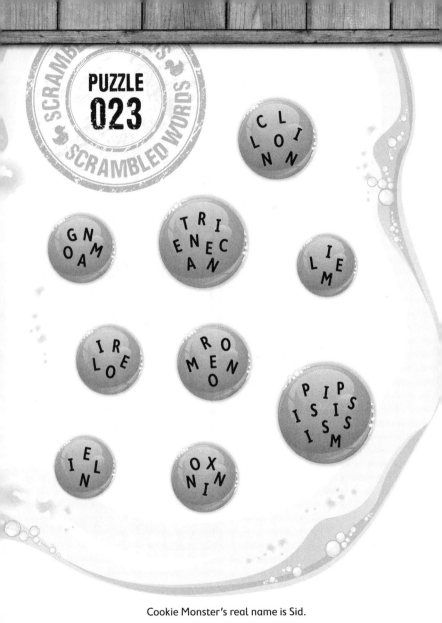

PUZZLE 023

Cookie Monster's real name is Sid.

	L	**M**	**N**
Rivers			
U.S. presidents			
Fruits			

Answers on page 262.

If you inhale a pea, it can sprout and grow in your lungs.

According to researchers at Newcastle University in the UK...

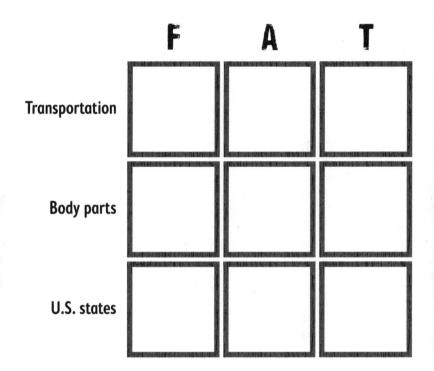

	F	**A**	**T**
Transportation			
Body parts			
U.S. states			

Answers on page 262.

...bacon sandwiches cure hangovers.

In 1918, more than 100 Chicago waiters were arrested for poisoning bad tippers.

	L	**P**	**S**
On the farm			
Footwear			
World cities			

Answers on page 262.

Play-Doh was originally created (in 1950) to clean coal residue off wallpaper.

SCRAMBLED WORDS
SCRAMBLED WORDS

V E
U A L

N H A
G

N S A
K E

N O
H D A

O V
O L V

O G
V L A

L S
E P E

O S
H D U
N

B A S
A

First country to seek diplomatic relations with the U.S.: Morocco (1777).

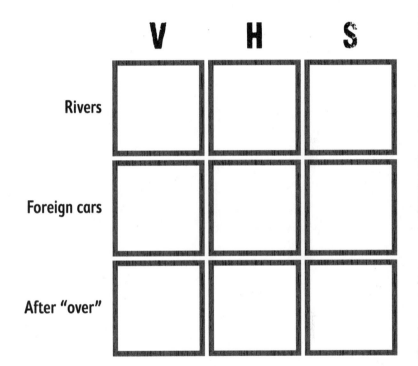

	V	**H**	**S**
Rivers			
Foreign cars			
After "over"			

Answers on page 263.

The periodic table of elements does not have the letter J on it.

SCRAMBLED WORDS
SCRAMBLED WORDS

K P C U

I E P N

W R D E O D O

E R W O P

E S E S N

R C U E P S

R E A C

A E T K S

I K N R

An Olympic shot put weighs the same as the maximum weight for a bowling ball.

54

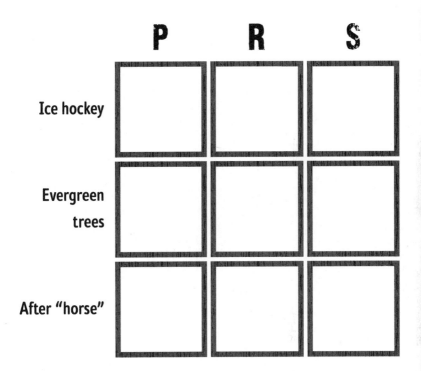

	P	**R**	**S**
Ice hockey			
Evergreen trees			
After "horse"			

Answers on page 263.

In Ireland, jack-o'-lanterns used to be carved from turnips.

SCRAMBLED WORDS

People from Nigeria are called "Nigerian." People from Niger are "Nigerien."

	S	**E**	**C**
On a ship			
Sea creatures			
Birds			

Answers on page 263.

Founding Fathers George Washington and Thomas Jefferson were both redheads.

NA
U D
S

A
N R
I

SV
T E
E N

A
N D
O R
L

A I
S
C A

V E
E R
N A

D I
R P
S E

N W
R A
N D
A

I K
N

Strawberry Shortcake started out as a greeting card character (1977).

	S	**I**	**R**
Countries			
They're black			
Men's names			

Answers on page 263.

Only mammals without bellybuttons: the platypus and the echidna.

Madonna's last name: Ciccone.

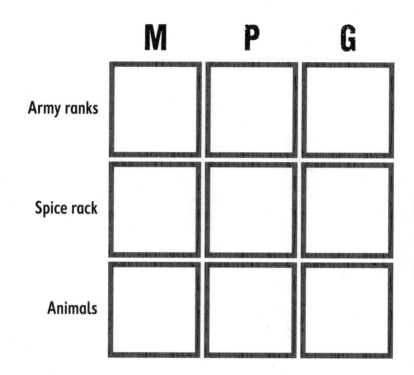

	M	**P**	**G**
Army ranks			
Spice rack			
Animals			

Answers on page 263.

At the North Pole, spit can freeze midair.

SCRAMBLED WORDS

Titles rejected by Pixar for the movie *Toy Story*...

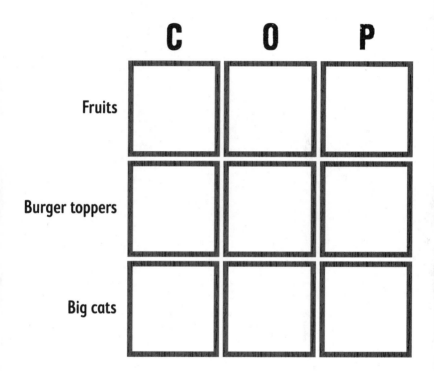

	C	**O**	**P**
Fruits			
Burger toppers			
Big cats			

Answers on page 264.

...Made in Taiwan, Moving Buddies, and *Toyz in the 'Hood.*

PUZZLE
032

Half of a computer byte is known as a "nibble."

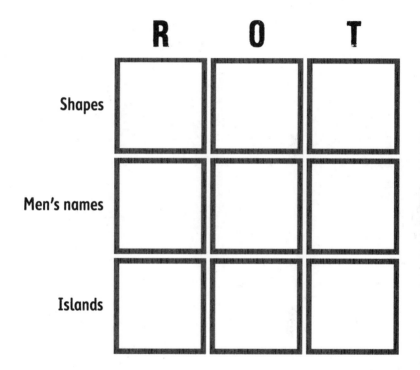

	R	**O**	**T**
Shapes			
Men's names			
Islands			

Answers on page 264.

Richard Nixon's favorite lunch: cottage cheese with ketchup.

The boys' teams at Centralia High School in Illinois are known as the Orphans...

	B	**A**	**N**
Books			
U.S. capitals			
Before "time"			

Answers on page 264.

...The girls' teams are the Annies.

PUZZLE 034

SCRAMBLED WORDS

- T I N A R O O E P
- U F E T L
- D F X E E
- X O R E X
- E O O B
- E P O S C R F
- A L O E R C
- A Y X R
- E L O O X H N P Y

The 1919 Stanley Cup was canceled due to the Spanish flu epidemic.

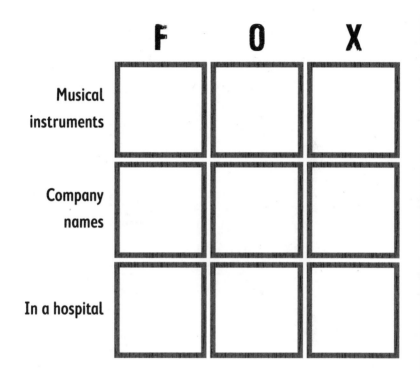

	F	**O**	**X**
Musical instruments			
Company names			
In a hospital			

Answers on page 264.

Only U.S. state where coffee is grown commercially: Hawaii.

PUZZLE
035

The NFL team with the longest-running cheerleading organization: Washington Redskins.

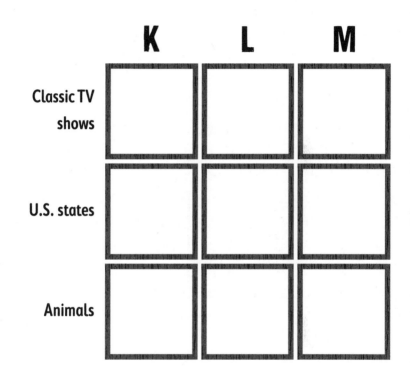

	K	**L**	**M**
Classic TV shows			
U.S. states			
Animals			

Answers on page 264.

Michael Jackson pitched an idea for a *Harry Potter* musical, but J. K. Rowling rejected it.

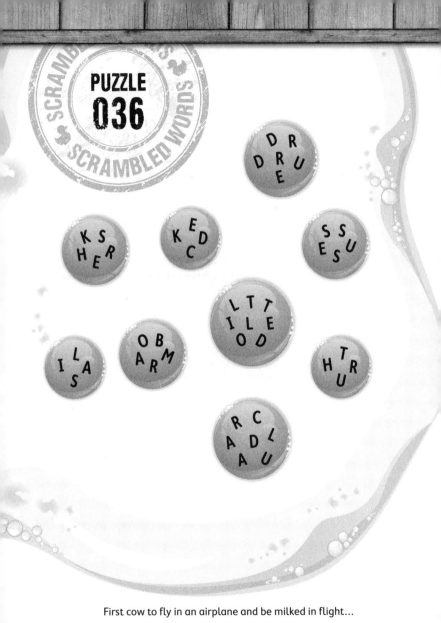

First cow to fly in an airplane and be milked in flight…

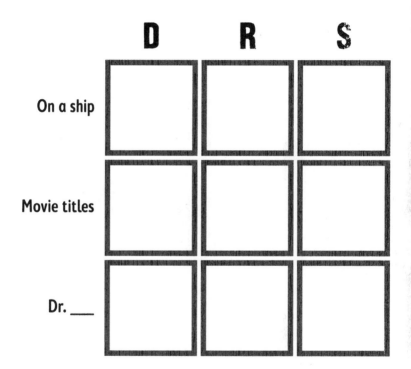

	D	R	S
On a ship			
Movie titles			
Dr. ___			

Answers on page 265.

...Missouri's Elm Farm Ollie (1930).

SCRAMBLED WORDS

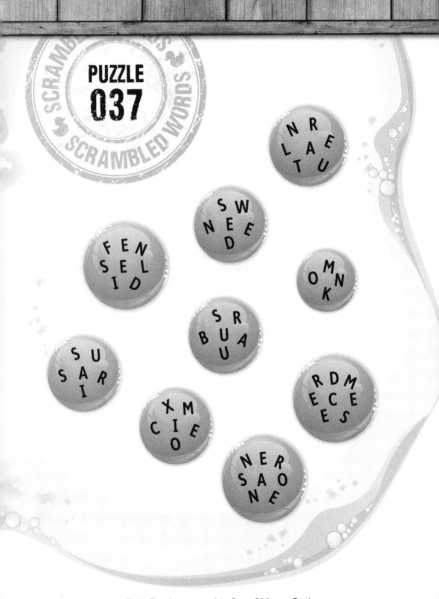

N R
L A E
T U

S W
N E E
D

F E N
S E L
I D

O M N
K

S R
B U A
U

S U
S A R
I

R D M
E C E
E S

X M
C I E
O

N E R
S A O
N E

Elvis Presley was a big fan of Monty Python.

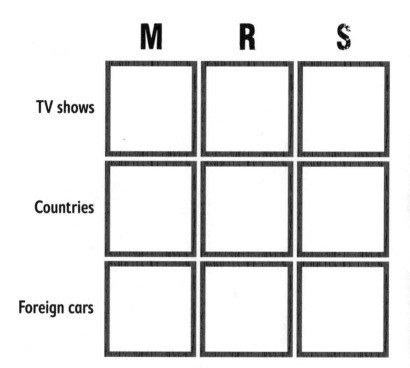

	M	**R**	**S**
TV shows			
Countries			
Foreign cars			

Answers on page 265.

"William Shakespeare" is an anagram of "I am a weakish speller."

PUZZLE 038

CH
R P E

N P
R I E
A S

L A
N M R
M I

A D S
P

N M
A X

C T I
K S

I D
A R N
E S

A S M
K

A E
I E S
M

The Library of Congress lists 72 different spellings for Moammar Gaddafi.

	M	**P**	**S**
Cat breeds			
Fish			
Hockey gear			

Answers on page 265.

Shortest player to lead the NBA in scoring: Allen Iverson (6').

SCRAMBLED WORDS
SCRAMBLED WORDS

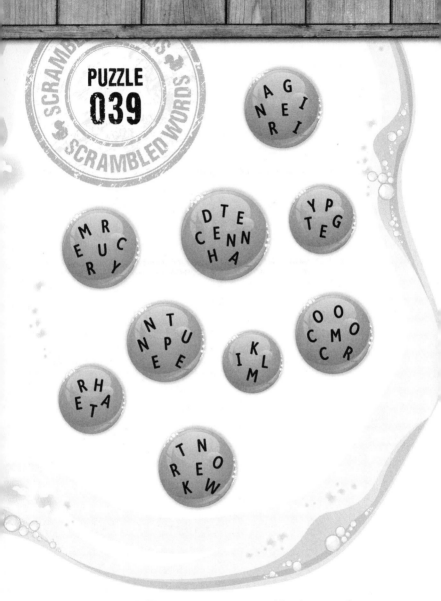

A G I
N R E I

M R E U C R Y

D T E C E N N H A

Y P T E G

N T P U E E

I K L M

O O C M O C R

R H E T A

T N R E O K W

All of Uranus's 27 known moons are named for characters from...

	M	**E**	**N**
African countries			
Movie titles			
Planets			

Answers on page 265.

...the works of William Shakespeare or Alexander Pope.

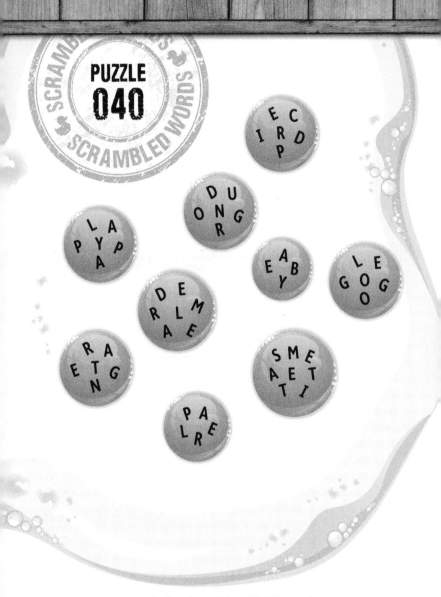

E C
I R D
P

D U
O N G
R

L A
P Y P
A

E A B
Y

L E
G O G
O

D E
R L M
A E

R A
E T G
N

S M E
A E T
T I

P A E
L R

An elephant's trunk has 150,000 muscles.

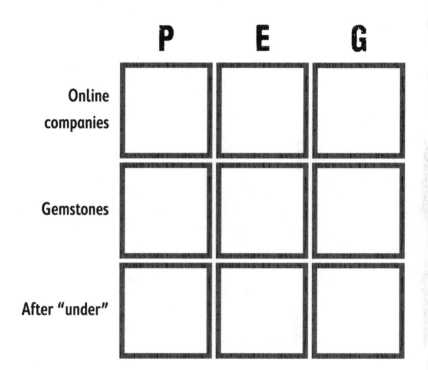

	P	E	G
Online companies			
Gemstones			
After "under"			

Answers on page 265.

John Tyler had the most children of any president: 15.

SCRAMBLED WORDS
SCRAMBLED WORDS

N A N E

H P E R C O S

A U A L P

N S N A I S

Y N L O N

I D A U

P R E T O E L Y S

Y N A N C

A R C L Y I C

World's leading exporter of beef: Australia.

	N	**A**	**P**
Synthetic fabrics			
Foreign cars			
Women's names			

Answers on page 266.

It would take a space shuttle 220 days to fly from the earth to the sun.

A B O T O

P U I R T N I R

E N R I H

H T E S M A

R Y R S O

H I P C N A S

A R H I D S

S R K I

I E E N S

The small protruding bump on the front of your ear is called a *tragus*.

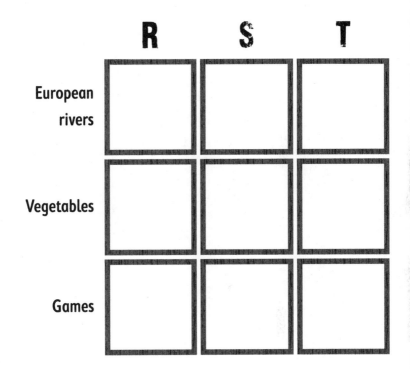

	R	**S**	**T**
European rivers			
Vegetables			
Games			

Answers on page 266.

U.S. nickels have more copper in them than pennies do.

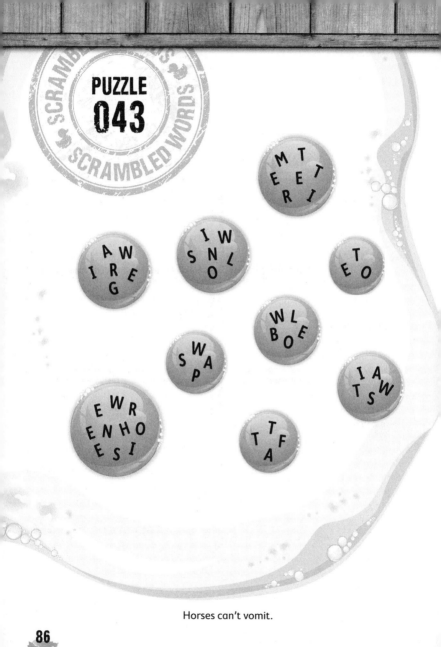

Horses can't vomit.

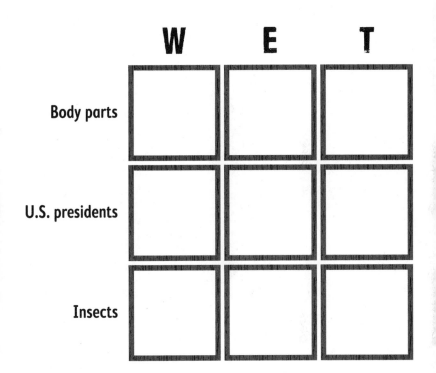

	W	**E**	**T**
Body parts			
U.S. presidents			
Insects			

Answers on page 266.

The world's leading exporter of false teeth: Liechtenstein.

Humans have taste receptors in their lungs.

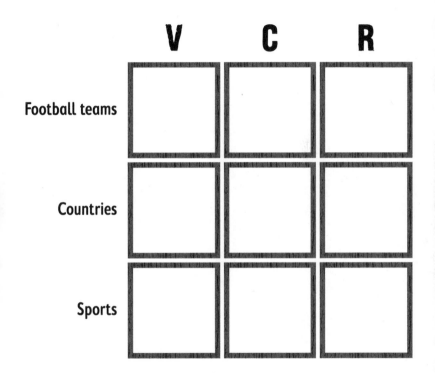

	V	**C**	**R**
Football teams			
Countries			
Sports			

Answers on page 266.

First nation to issue adhesive postage stamps: Great Britain (1840).

SCRAMBLED WORDS
SCRAMBLED WORDS

I T N

N R I O

R S I T N E E T

T L E L R E

T P R L I

A C S H

I N N I N G

P O R C E E

C T C H A

The Rose Bowl was originally called the "Battle of the Flowers."

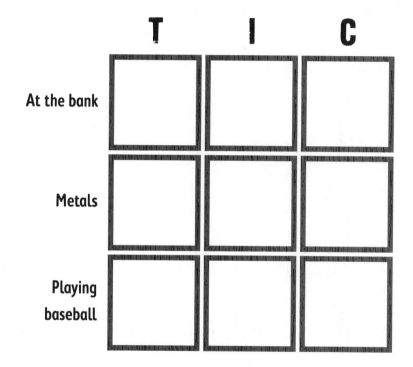

	T	I	C
At the bank			
Metals			
Playing baseball			

Answers on page 266.

An overdose on caffeine can cause hallucinations.

Thomas Edison's last breath is stored in a test tube...

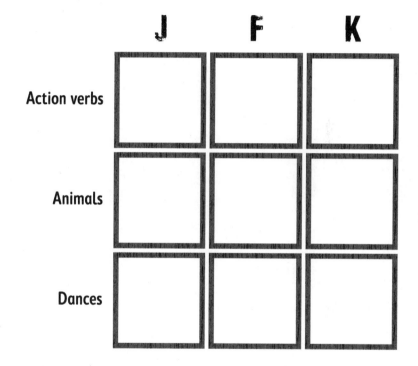

	J	F	K
Action verbs			
Animals			
Dances			

Answers on page 267.

...at the Henry Ford Museum in Dearborn, MI.

Only state that ends with the letter G: Wyoming.

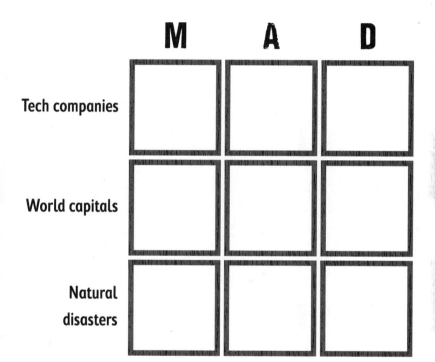

M   A   D

	M	A	D
Tech companies			
World capitals			
Natural disasters			

Answers on page 267.

Tobacco ads were banned from U.S. television in 1971.

First U.S. president to brew beer in the White House: Barack Obama.

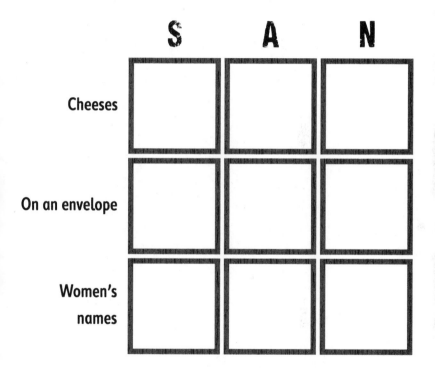

	S	A	N
Cheeses			
On an envelope			
Women's names			

Answers on page 267.

Q. What state has the longest coastline in the lower 48? A. Michigan.

Sir Paul McCartney's actual first name is James.

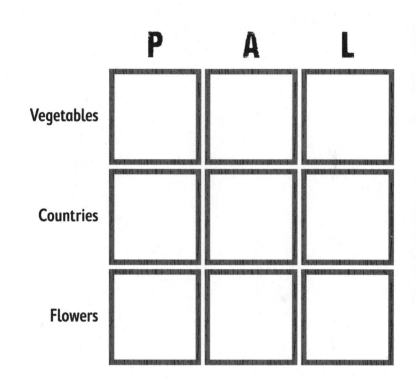

	P	**A**	**L**
Vegetables			
Countries			
Flowers			

Answers on page 267.

Napoleon's horse Marengo outlived him by eight years.

PUZZLE 050

The NFL's Green Bay Packers were named for the...

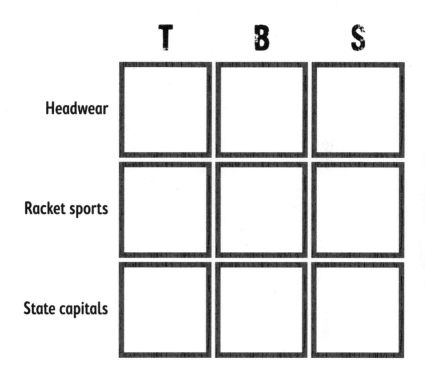

	T	B	S
Headwear			
Racket sports			
State capitals			

Answers on page 267.

...Indian Packing Company, which gave the team $500 to buy equipment.

EXTRA CIRCLE

If you look closely at the following pages, you'll see the basic 3 x 3 grid but...what's this? Nine squares and *ten* circles? In this section, you have the added challenge of figuring out which set of circled letters is a red herring and can't be unscrambled to produce a word.

PUZZLE
051

Figure out which one of the ten circles contains letters that can't be unscrambled to produce a word. Then figure out where the other unscrambled words go in the grid.

O N O L

G N N E V

N R E T

A S L I

G U L N

L A L E

Y E E

M U E

H G T H I

M Y T A M

In 1998, a Georgia high school student was suspended for...

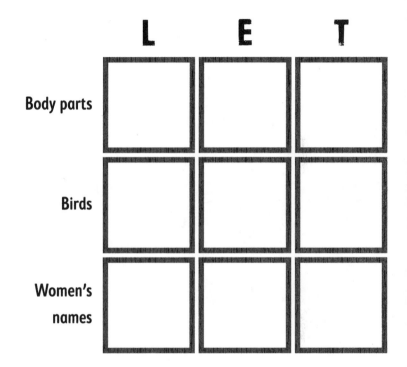

	L	**E**	**T**
Body parts			
Birds			
Women's names			

Answers on page 268.

...wearing a Pepsi shirt on "Coke in Education Day."

Figure out which one of the ten circles contains letters that can't be unscrambled to produce a word. Then figure out where the other unscrambled words go in the grid.

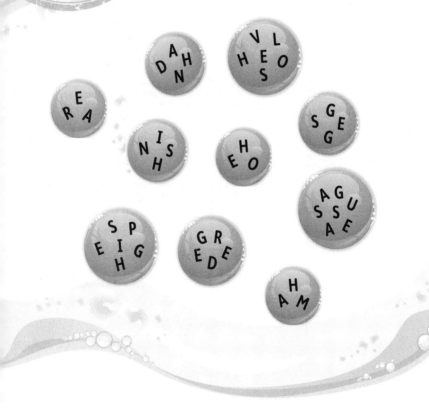

A female ferret is known as a "jill."

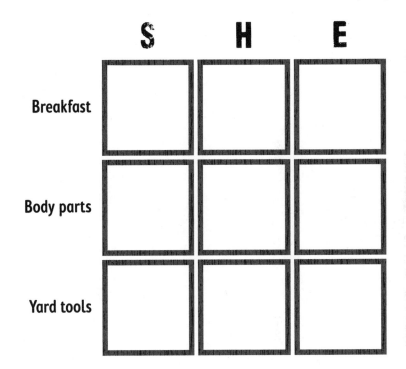

	S	H	E
Breakfast			
Body parts			
Yard tools			

Answers on page 268.

Construction of the Pentagon began on September 11, 1941.

PUZZLE
053

Figure out which one of the ten circles contains letters that can't be unscrambled to produce a word. Then figure out where the other unscrambled words go in the grid.

B E O L B G

C H M A R

L A B S I

T N M I

K A R B

T H B I R

L A I G C

M E R Y G

M E M B

O O

Philosopher René Descartes was attracted to cross-eyed women.

108

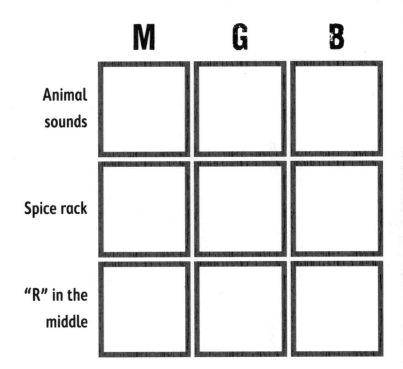

	M	**G**	**B**
Animal sounds			
Spice rack			
"R" in the middle			

Answers on page 268.

In the 1920s, Kool-Aid's official name was Fruit Smack.

Figure out which one of the ten circles contains letters that can't be unscrambled to produce a word. Then figure out where the other unscrambled words go in the grid.

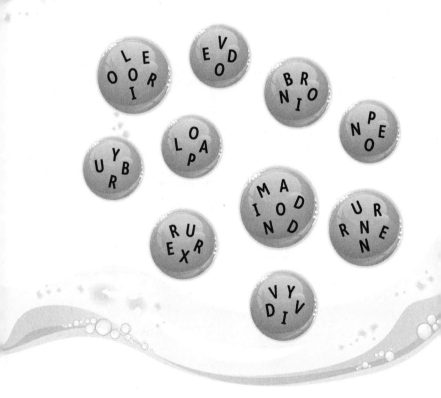

Actor John Cazale appeared in only five films during his entire career...

	R	**O**	**D**
Before "up"			
Gemstones			
Birds			

Answers on page 268.

...all of them were nominated for or won a Best Picture Oscar.

Figure out which one of the ten circles contains letters that can't be unscrambled to produce a word. Then figure out where the other unscrambled words go in the grid.

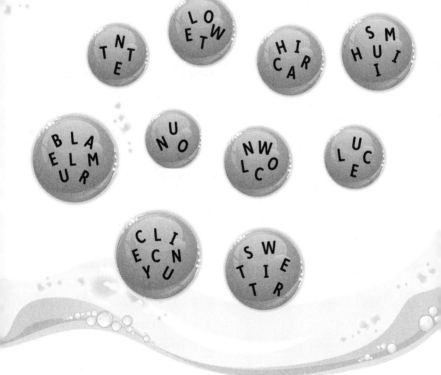

Technical name for crash-test dummies: anthropomorphic test device.

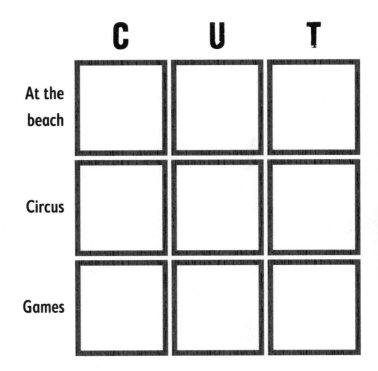

	C	**U**	**T**
At the beach			
Circus			
Games			

Answers on page 268.

Facebook engineers originally wanted to call the "Like" button the "Awesome" button.

PUZZLE 056

SCRAMBLED WORDS SCRAMBLED WORDS

Figure out which one of the ten circles contains letters that can't be unscrambled to produce a word. Then figure out where the other unscrambled words go in the grid.

V E L L E

D R I B U

R E M H M A

C R L K E O

L A H L H

E D K S

L R L I D

L A M A L

Y E D O N K

S H O R E

The "blood" used in the famous shower scene in Hitchcock's...

114

	D	**H**	**L**
Pack animals			
In a school			
Tools			

Answers on page 269.

...Psycho was actually chocolate syrup.

Figure out which one of the ten circles contains letters that can't be unscrambled to produce a word. Then figure out where the other unscrambled words go in the grid.

T R E B E

D R A E B

B Y D E R

G O D E D

G H O T U U N D

A P C

C U K I B

S L Y R E R C H

P E A U C C K

P A M E M

Printer ink costs seven times more per milliliter than Dom Perignon champagne.

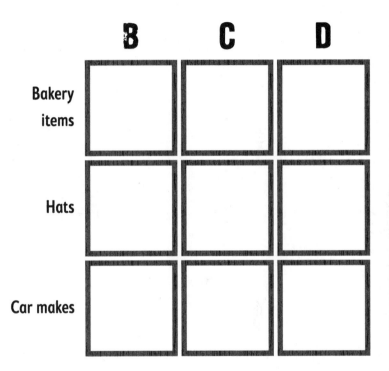

	B	C	D
Bakery items			
Hats			
Car makes			

Answers on page 269.

There is a doctor in Laguna Beach, CA, who can turn brown eyes permanently blue.

Figure out which one of the ten circles contains letters that can't be unscrambled to produce a word. Then figure out where the other unscrambled words go in the grid.

SCRAMBLED WORDS
SCRAMBLED WORDS

A T R B I B

D A T O

L E T P O A N E

S E O R

T E A S R

C Y K R O

P L T I U

N E L A I

B I E B B

R Y O T

Somewhere in the world, a language dies every two weeks.

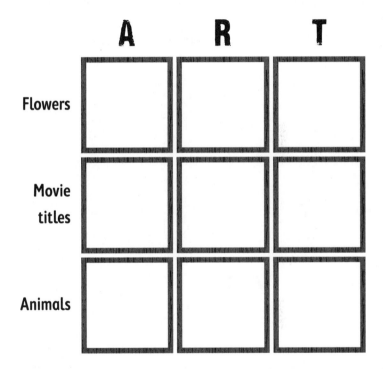

	A	**R**	**T**
Flowers			
Movie titles			
Animals			

Answers on page 269.

Studies show: The octopus is the most intelligent invertebrate.

Figure out which one of the ten circles contains letters that can't be unscrambled to produce a word. Then figure out where the other unscrambled words go in the grid.

K O S P E

G O R P O

L A D E P

K A B E R

T E B

C I E A L N P

K O R P E

Y O O B B

R A O R P S W

O L T S S

The band Styx released its album *The Grand Illusion* on 7/7/77.

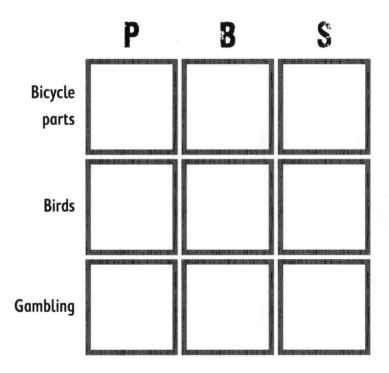

	P	B	S
Bicycle parts			
Birds			
Gambling			

Answers on page 269.

Charles Darwin and Abraham Lincoln were born on the same day: February 12, 1809.

PUZZLE 060

Figure out which one of the ten circles contains letters that can't be unscrambled to produce a word. Then figure out where the other unscrambled words go in the grid.

S L S A A

H L C I I

C A T O

O I L S

P R L U E X

C A R R O T T

L S E H L

N O R C V H E

W O C

C A E X T O

Average lifespan of a major-league baseball: seven pitches.

122

	C	T	S
Gas stations			
Mexican food			
On the farm			

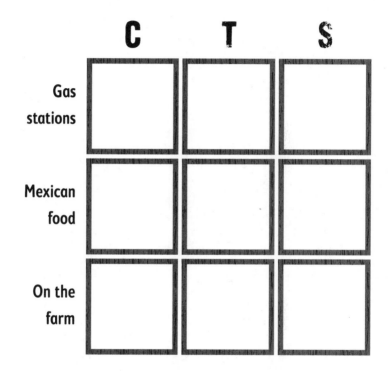

Answers on page 269.

Aging male giraffes go black, not gray.

Figure out which one of the ten circles contains letters that can't be unscrambled to produce a word. Then figure out where the other unscrambled words go in the grid.

In 1978, you could buy shampoo with real beer in it...

	S	T	P
Candy brands			
European countries			
Fabrics			

Answers on page 270.

...It was called Body on Tap.

PUZZLE 062

Figure out which one of the ten circles contains letters that can't be unscrambled to produce a word. Then figure out where the other unscrambled words go in the grid.

U A B R A

H A S

S P E Y S C R

O W R C

A H I T I

C H P A E A

I O P H

L Y O L H

B A U C

C R L B U

The largest collection of Christian relics outside of the Vatican is in Pittsburgh.

126

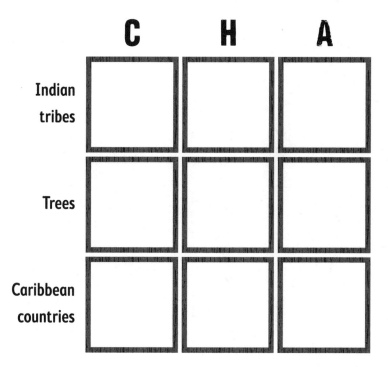

	C	H	A
Indian tribes			
Trees			
Caribbean countries			

Answers on page 270.

Bill Clinton sent only two emails during his two terms as president.

Figure out which one of the ten circles contains letters that can't be unscrambled to produce a word. Then figure out where the other unscrambled words go in the grid.

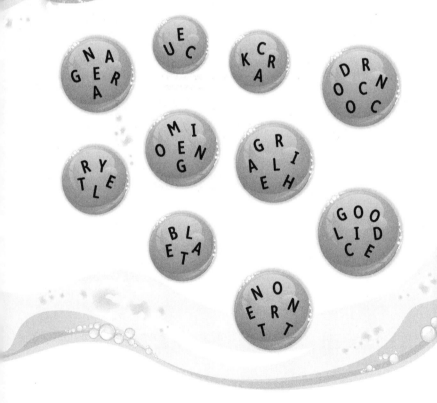

Sir Arthur Conan Doyle helped popularize skiing in Switzerland.

	C	**R**	**T**
Billiards			
U.S. presidents			
State capitals			

Answers on page 270.

Box jellyfish have eyes but no brains.

Figure out which one of the ten circles contains letters that can't be unscrambled to produce a word. Then figure out where the other unscrambled words go in the grid.

A E C H R G

P D A

S P S A

V U I N N

L E A E S

S V N A A C

E I L S V

R C E H

C I E R P N

X E P S E O

The peacock is actually the male name of the peafowl...

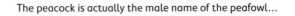

	P	**E**	**C**
Art supplies			
One-named singers			
Follows "over"			

Answers on page 270.

...Females are called peahens.

Figure out which one of the ten circles contains letters that can't be unscrambled to produce a word. Then figure out where the other unscrambled words go in the grid.

L O W
F

L I D
A R L M
O A

I E N
A N

T R
A A E
C B

P I
M H C

T A N
U

S O
U C I
N

C E
W I D
K

C M I
P E

E I F
W

Aardvark is Afrikaans for "earth pig."

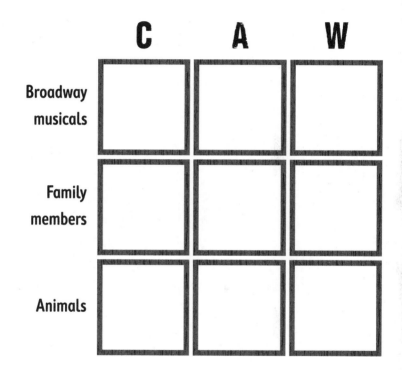

	C	**A**	**W**
Broadway musicals			
Family members			
Animals			

Answers on page 270.

Only U.S. president to serve two nonconsecutive terms: Grover Cleveland.

Figure out which one of the ten circles contains letters that can't be unscrambled to produce a word. Then figure out where the other unscrambled words go in the grid.

L I L D

K C H E C

T E S I D O P

S G L I P

M N I D E

V H E I C

O N O C T T

U D S E E

O S F F N A

E A F S

First baseball player to receive a million-dollar salary: Nolan Ryan, Houston Astros (1979).

	C	**D**	**S**
Banking			
Spice rack			
Fabrics			

Answers on page 271.

Parents in Denmark must have their new child's name approved by the government.

PUZZLE 067

Figure out which one of the ten circles contains letters that can't be unscrambled to produce a word. Then figure out where the other unscrambled words go in the grid.

I A W I H I H A

R H T Z E

N D R E E V

E D L A A W E R

N O L U U H O L

H H L E O M

N L T T A A A

O D L A L R

I V S A

S A A K L

In the mid-19th century, gasoline was sold in small bottles as a cure for lice.

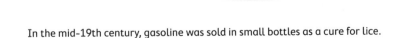

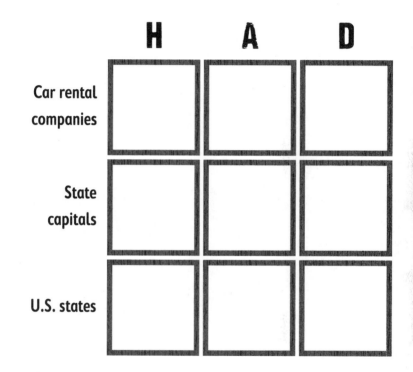

	H	**A**	**D**
Car rental companies			
State capitals			
U.S. states			

Answers on page 271.

Duct tape was developed during WWII as a waterproof seal for boxes of ammunition.

Figure out which one of the ten circles contains letters that can't be unscrambled to produce a word. Then figure out where the other unscrambled words go in the grid.

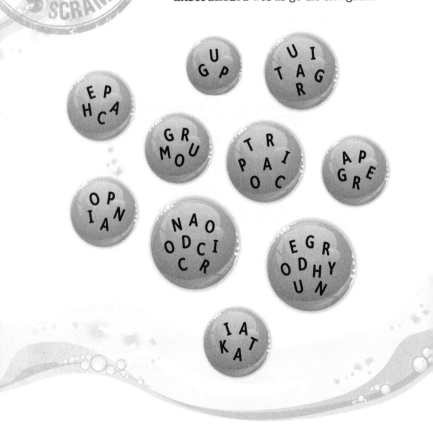

More people have traveled to the moon than to the deepest part of the ocean.

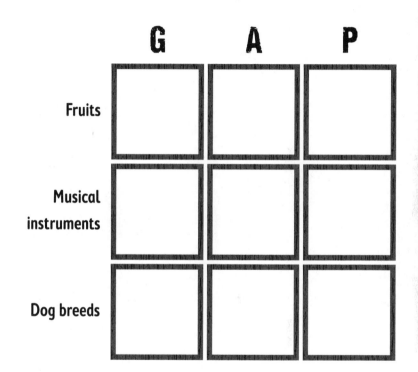

	G	**A**	**P**
Fruits			
Musical instruments			
Dog breeds			

Answers on page 271.

The web URL letters "http" stand for "hypertext transfer protocol."

Figure out which one of the ten circles contains letters that can't be unscrambled to produce a word. Then figure out where the other unscrambled words go in the grid.

A N M O

K D A M E R N

M I O L P Y A

D R O R E

D R V E E

M D I O S N A

I A M L

E T D A

V D O R E

C H T M A

John Lennon's 1975 single "Number 9 Dream" peaked...

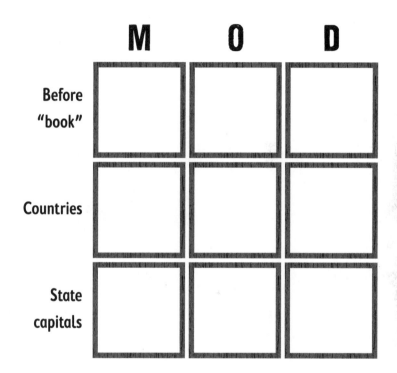

	M	**O**	**D**
Before "book"			
Countries			
State capitals			

Answers on page 271.

...on the billboard charts at number nine.

Figure out which one of the ten circles contains letters that can't be unscrambled to produce a word. Then figure out where the other unscrambled words go in the grid.

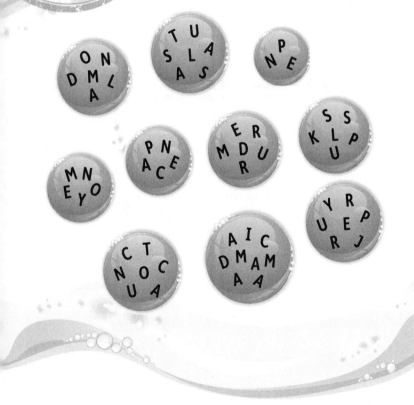

O N D M L A

T U S L A S

N P E

E R M D U R

S S K L P U

P N A C E

M N E Y O

Y R U E P R J

C T N O C U A

A I C D M A M A A

Celebrity chef Julia Child was 6'2".

142

	M	**A**	**P**
At the bank			
Crimes			
Nuts			

Answers on page 271.

Orangutan is from the Malay, meaning "man of the forest."

PUZZLE 071

Figure out which one of the ten circles contains letters that can't be unscrambled to produce a word. Then figure out where the other unscrambled words go in the grid.

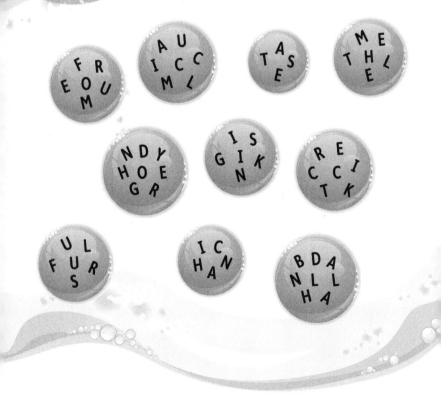

Michelangelo died in 1564, the same year Shakespeare was born.

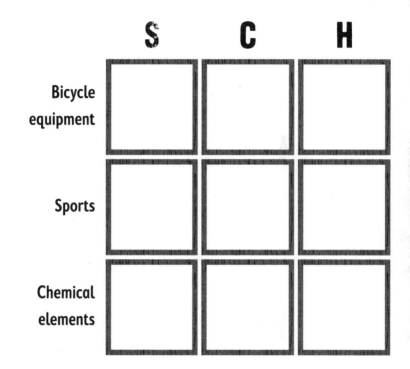

	S	**C**	**H**
Bicycle equipment			
Sports			
Chemical elements			

Answers on page 272.

Rejected name for what became Washington State: Columbia.

Figure out which one of the ten circles contains letters that can't be unscrambled to produce a word. Then figure out where the other unscrambled words go in the grid.

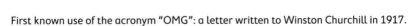
First known use of the acronym "OMG": a letter written to Winston Churchill in 1917.

	M	**T**	**V**
World cities			
Musical instruments			
Birds			

Answers on page 272.

Technically, fireflies are not flies—they're beetles.

PUZZLE
073

Figure out which one of the ten circles contains letters that can't be unscrambled to produce a word. Then figure out where the other unscrambled words go in the grid.

Former NBA player Dikembe Mutombo speaks English, French, Spanish...

	S	O	N
Chemical elements			
Indian tribes			
Animals			

Answers on page 272.

...Portuguese, and five African languages.

SCRAMBLED WORDS
SCRAMBLED WORDS

Figure out which one of the ten circles contains letters that can't be unscrambled to produce a word. Then figure out where the other unscrambled words go in the grid.

H O R
E L T
O P

M A E
L

L Y A
P

A M S
T

A L
K O P

G A R

M E A
A A C
N R

E P R
O

G P
E T L
U

U R M
A B

Elvis had an identical twin brother who died at birth.

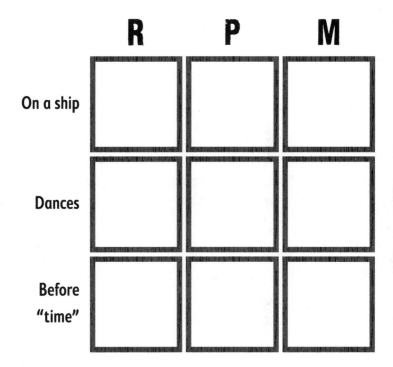

	R	**P**	**M**
On a ship			
Dances			
Before "time"			

Answers on page 272.

Horses can't breathe through their mouths.

PUZZLE 075

Figure out which one of the ten circles contains letters that can't be unscrambled to produce a word. Then figure out where the other unscrambled words go in the grid.

Circles:

Y M T H E

A I L A V L N

E S A H P X O O N

M R H U O T

H S H R U T

P M T E R U T

N I L I O V

G E A S

Y E V E R

L W L S A O W

Canadian pediatrician Henri Breault invented the child-resistant medicine cap in 1967.

152

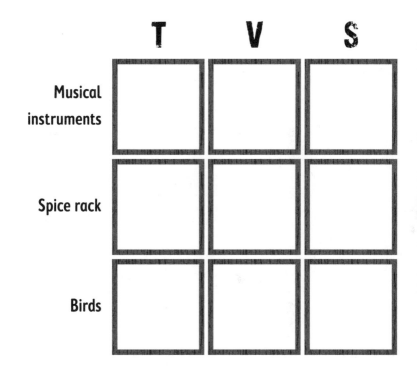

	T	V	S
Musical instruments			
Spice rack			
Birds			

Answers on page 272.

Only sign of the zodiac represented by an inanimate object: Libra (scales).

MISSING CATEGORY

Nine circles and nine squares—so far, so good. But this time, there's a blank where one of the categories should be. First unscramble all the words from the letters in the circles and fit the ones you can into the correct squares. Then, by process of elimination, you should be able to figure out what the missing category is.

PUZZLE 076

Figure out what the missing category is and write it in the blank.

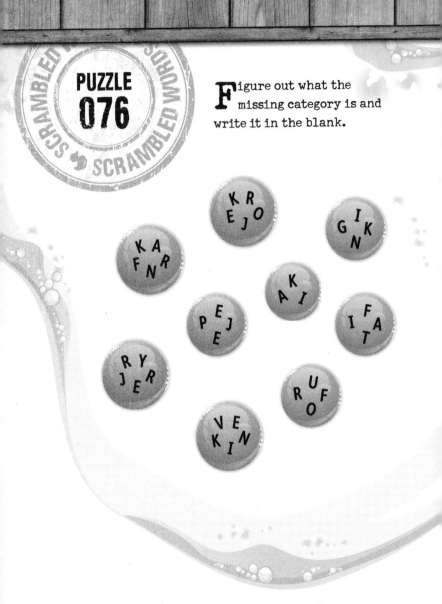

Despite being only 2% of our body mass, our brains...

	J	**F**	**K**
Playing cards			
Men's names			
_____			

Answers on page 273.

...use 20% of our daily caloric intake.

PUZZLE 077

Figure out what the missing category is and write it in the blank.

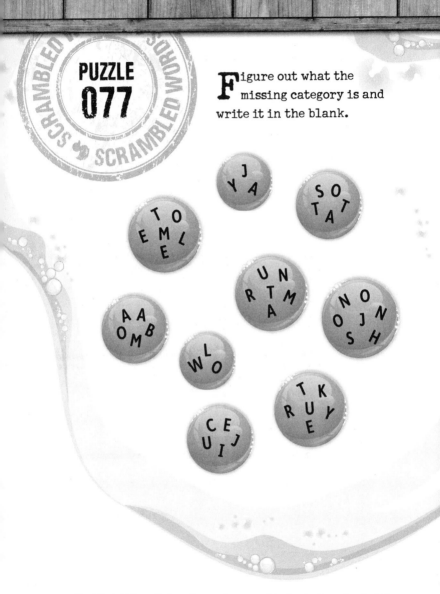

The World Chess Federation performs antidoping tests on its players.

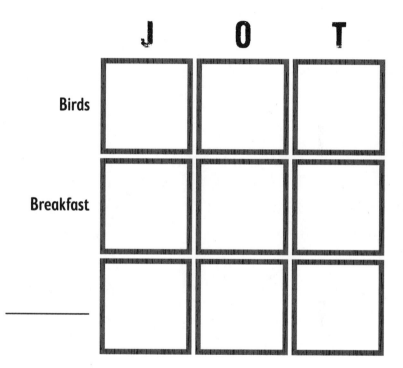

	J	**O**	**T**
Birds			
Breakfast			
_____			

Answers on page 273.

The *Apollo 11* computers had less processing power than a modern cell phone.

Figure out what the missing category is and write it in the blank.

SA
P

VO
BA
R

AC
BRO

TN
A

GR
CHE
A

YO
AH

OB
A

TR
CIE
KC

BE
E

Before George W. Bush took office as president, Clinton administration pranksters...

	A	**B**	**C**
Yelled words			
Insects			
_____			

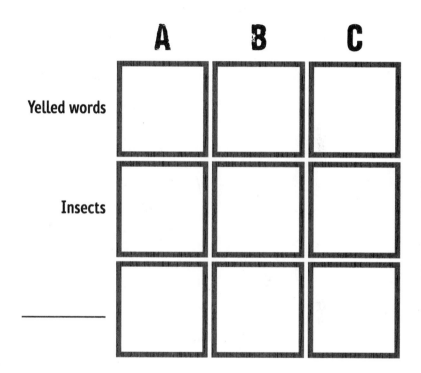

Answers on page 273.

...removed the Ws from White House computer keyboards.

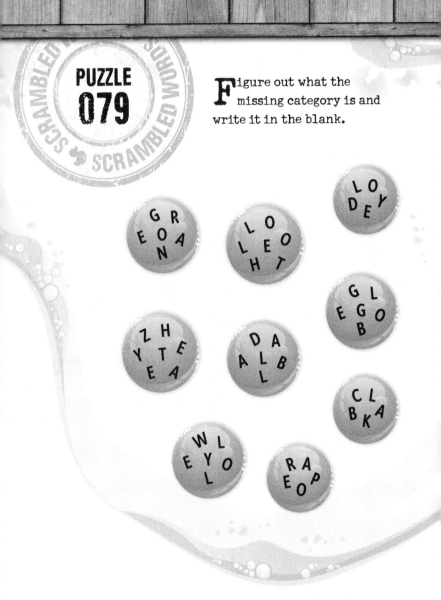

Figure out what the missing category is and write it in the blank.

During WWII, La-Z-Boy manufactured seats for tanks.

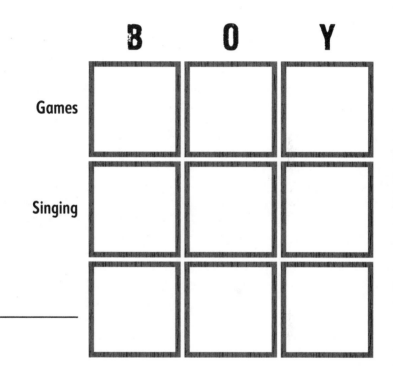

	B	**O**	**Y**
Games			
Singing			
_____			

Answers on page 273.

There was once a lake the size of England in the Sahara.

Figure out what the missing category is and write it in the blank.

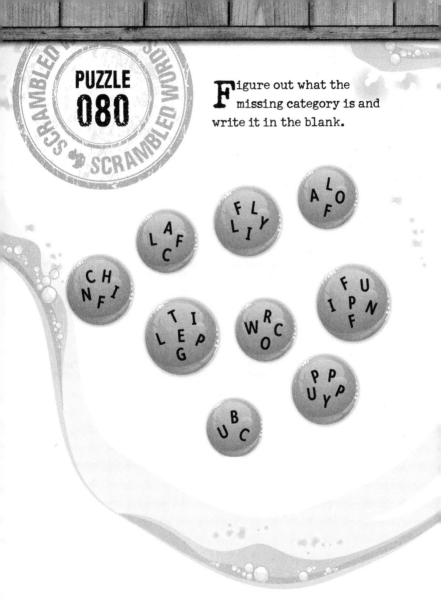

Only U.S. state flag with a green background: Washington.

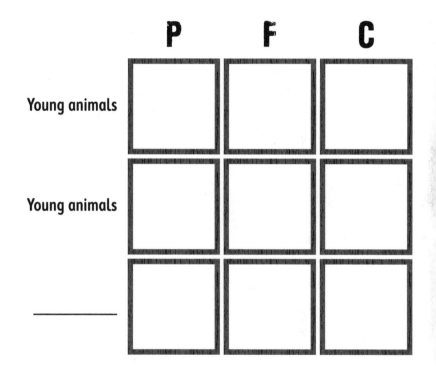

	P	**F**	**C**
Young animals			
Young animals			
_____			

Answers on page 273.

Kiribati is the only country to lie in all four hemispheres.

Figure out what the missing category is and write it in the blank.

N E A
Y H

R O F
G

U Z F
Z

D O
U G N
R

R I H
A

R O
E E G
G

E X I
F L

P H
G E R
O

D R
W A O
H

Only U.S. state to border just one other state: Maine.

	F	**G**	**H**
Before "ball"			
Men's names			
_____			

Answers on page 274.

Wombats have cube-shaped poop.

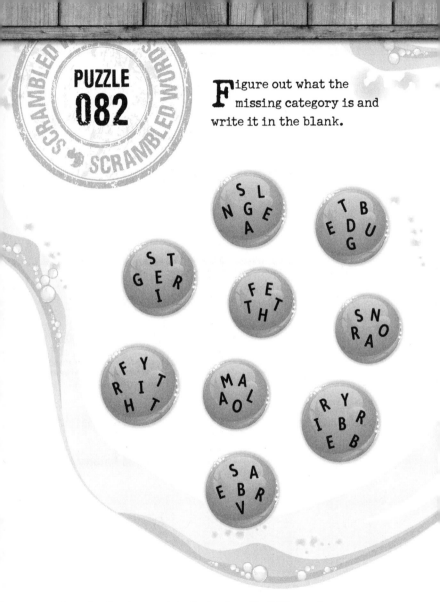

Figure out what the missing category is and write it in the blank.

S L
N G E
A

T B
E D U
G

S T
G E R
I

F E
T H T

S N
R A O

F Y
R I T
H I T

M A
A O L

R Y
I B R
E B

S A
E B R
V

Hawaiian Punch was originally developed in 1934 as an ice cream syrup.

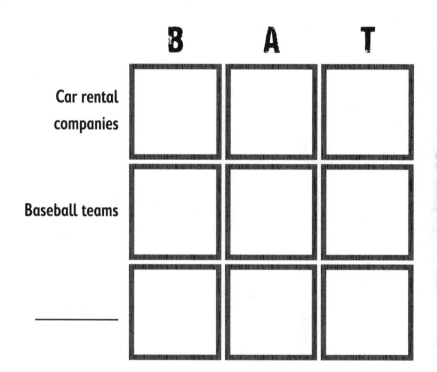

	B	A	T
Car rental companies			
Baseball teams			
_____			

Answers on page 274.

Q. What's Shaggy's real name in the *Scooby Doo* cartoons? A. Norville Rogers.

PUZZLE 083

Figure out what the missing category is and write it in the blank.

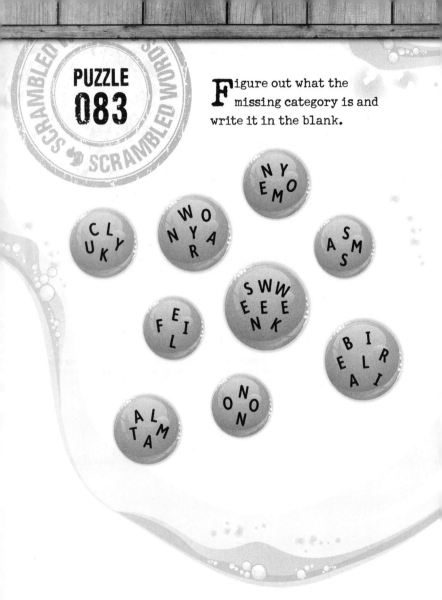

Longest word that can be typed using letters on only one row of the keyboard: typewriter.

170

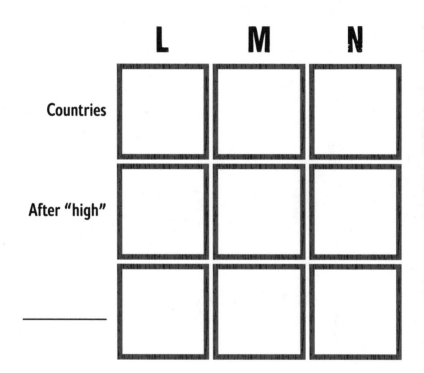

	L	**M**	**N**
Countries			
After "high"			
_____			

Answers on page 274.

Two dogs were executed for witchcraft during the Salem witch trials.

Figure out what the missing category is and write it in the blank.

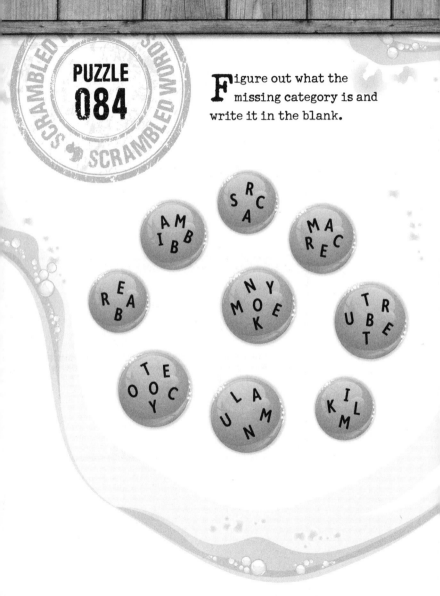

S R C A

A M I B B

M A R E C

R E A B

N Y M O E K

T R U B E T

T E O O C Y

L A U M N

K I L M

The "Q" in "Q-Tips" stands for "quality."

	B	**M**	**C**
Animals			
Animated movies			
_____			

Answers on page 274.

Last U.S. president to sport a mustache: William Howard Taft.

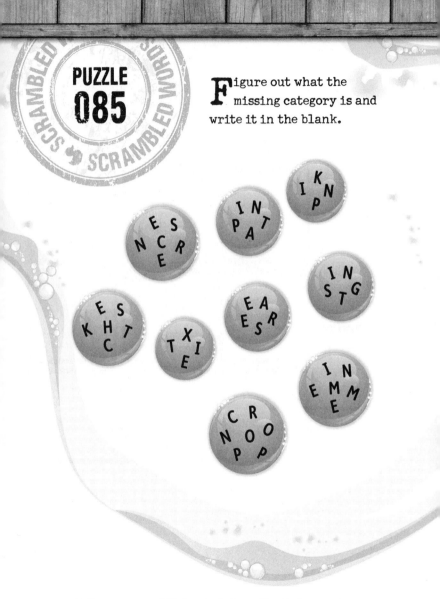

Figure out what the missing category is and write it in the blank.

Q: How can you tell if already-foul-smelling Limburger cheese...

	E	S	P
Creating art			
In a movie theater			
_____			

Answers on page 274.

...has gone bad? A: It starts to smell like ammonia.

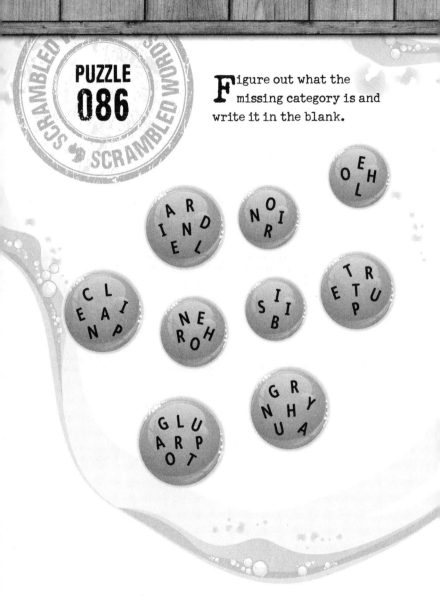

PUZZLE 086

Figure out what the missing category is and write it in the blank.

O E H
O L

A R
I N
D
E L

N O I
R

T R
E T U
P

C L I
E
A
N P

N E
R O H

S I I
B

G R
N H Y
U A

G L U
A R P
O T

John Newton, composer of "Amazing Grace," was a reformed slave trader.

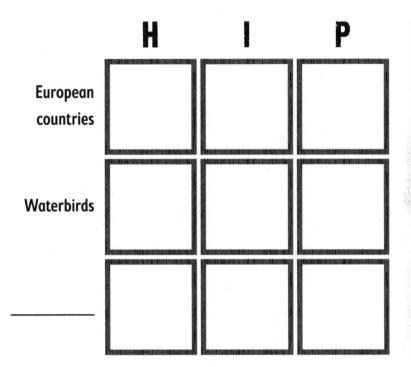

	H	**I**	**P**
European countries			
Waterbirds			
_____			

Answers on page 275.

Original title of Arthur Miller's *Death of a Salesman*: *The Inside of His Head*.

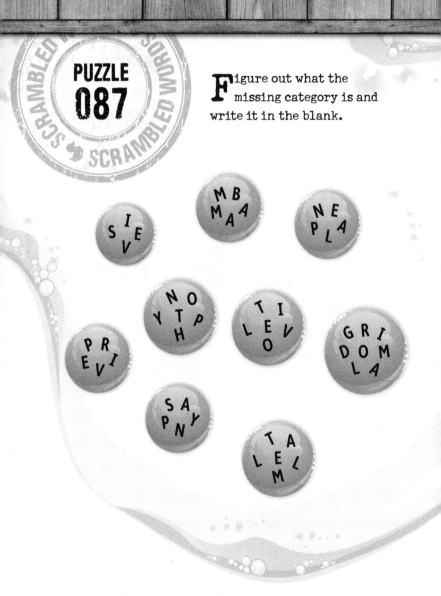

Figure out what the missing category is and write it in the blank.

SIEV

MBMAA

NELAP

NOTYPH

TILEVO

GRIDOMLA

PREVI

SAPNY

TALELM

Bubble gum is pink because it was the only...

	M	**V**	**P**
Flowers			
Tools			
_____			

Answers on page 275.

...color of dye that inventor Walter E. Diemer had on hand.

Figure out what the missing category is and write it in the blank.

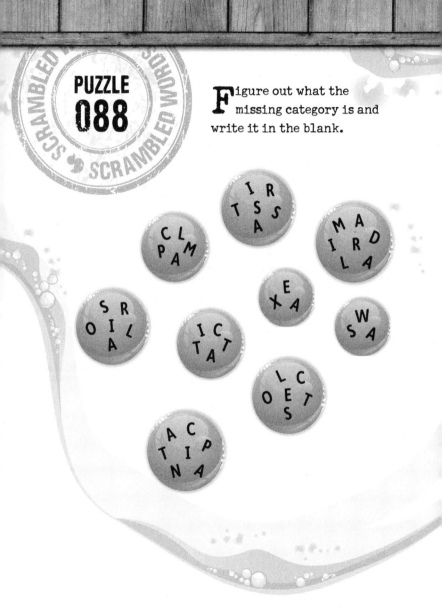

Oldest Beatle: Ringo (born July 7, 1940).

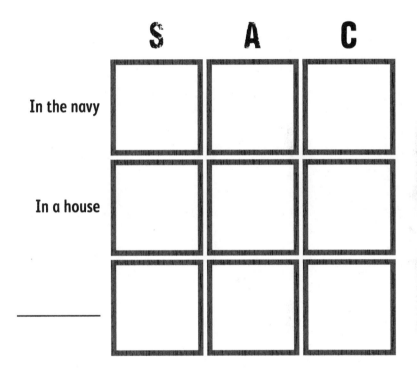

	S	**A**	**C**
In the navy			
In a house			
_____			

Answers on page 275.

Ben Franklin had no formal education beyond age ten.

SCRAMBLED WORDS · SCRAMBLED WORDS

Figure out what the missing category is and write it in the blank.

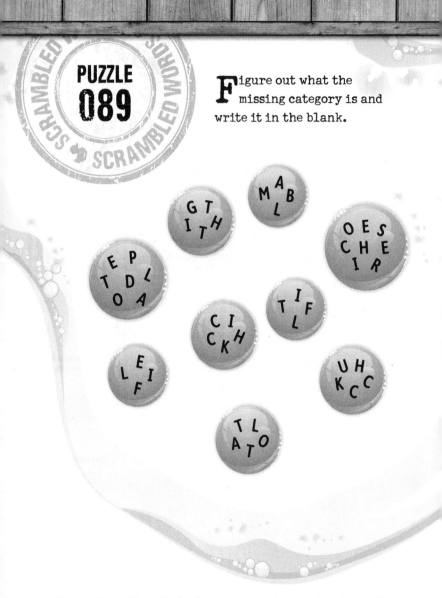

- G T I T H
- M A B L
- O E S C H E I R
- E P T D L O A
- T I F L
- C I C K H
- L E I F
- U H K C C
- T L A T O

Homer Hickam's book *Rocket Boys* was adapted into the film *October Sky*…

	T	**L**	**C**
Young animals			
After "up"			
_____			

Answers on page 275.

...The titles are anagrams of each other.

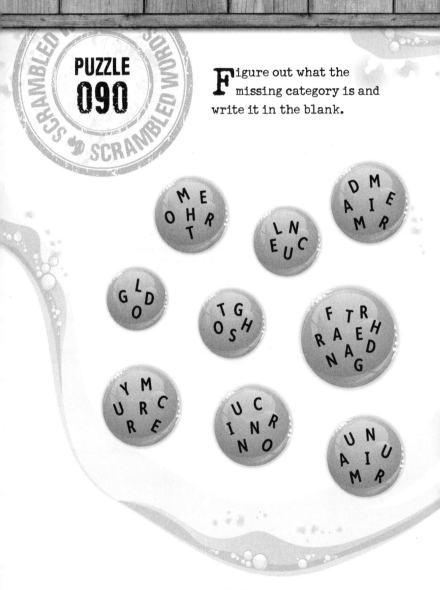

PUZZLE 090

Figure out what the missing category is and write it in the blank.

M E O H T R

L N E U C

D M A I E M R

G L D O

T G O S H

F T R R A E H N A D G

Y M U R R C E

U C I N R O N

U N A I U M R

Camels originated in North America.

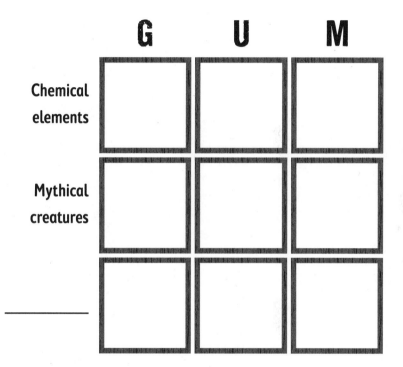

	G	**U**	**M**
Chemical elements			
Mythical creatures			
_____			

Answers on page 275.

The average strawberry contains 200 seeds.

SCRAMBLED WORDS · SCRAMBLED WORDS

Figure out what the missing category is and write it in the blank.

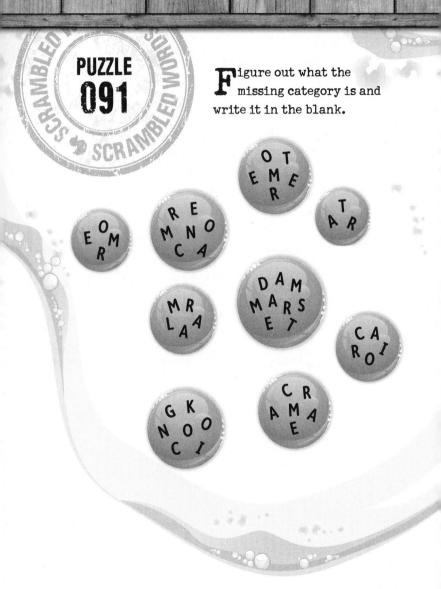

Both the Howard Johnson's and Dunkin' Donuts chains were founded in Massachusetts.

	C	**A**	**R**
Battery-powered			
Bookstore sections			
_____			

Answers on page 276.

Red M&Ms were discontinued from 1976 to 1985 when the FDA banned Red Dye No. 2.

F igure out what the missing category is and write it in the blank.

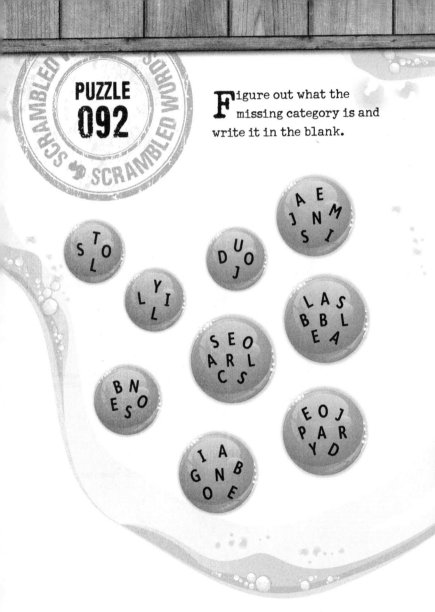

S T O L

L Y I L

D U O J

J A E N M S I

L A S B B L E A

S E O A R L C S

B N E S O

E O J P A R Y D

I A G N B O E

People used to chew willow bark as a pain reliever.

	L	**B**	**J**
Flowers			
TV shows			
_____			

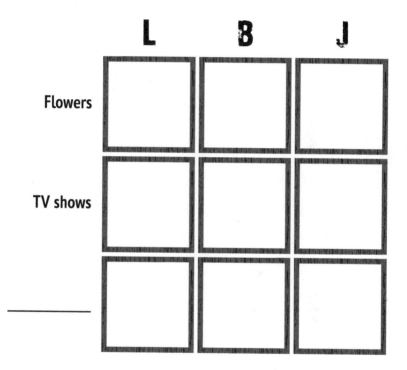

Answers on page 276.

You can make paper out of dryer lint.

Figure out what the missing category is and write it in the blank.

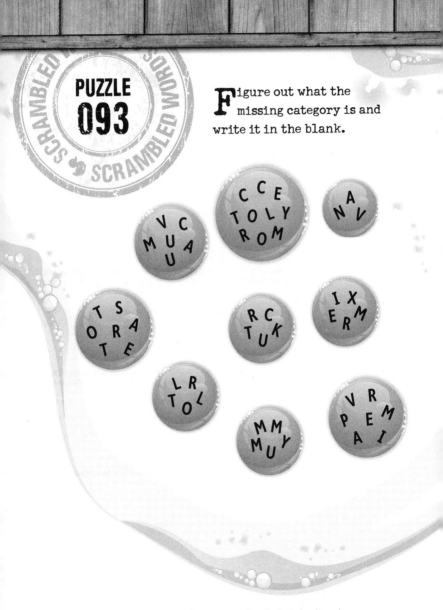

V C
M U U A
U

C C E
T O L Y
R O M

N A V

T S
O R A
T E E

R C
T U K

I X
E R M
R

L R
T O L

M M
M U Y

V R
P E M
A I

Only countries whose names begin, but don't end...

	M	**T**	**V**
Mythical creatures			
Appliances			
_____			

Answers on page 276.

... with the letter A: Afghanistan and Azerbaijan.

Figure out what the missing category is and write it in the blank.

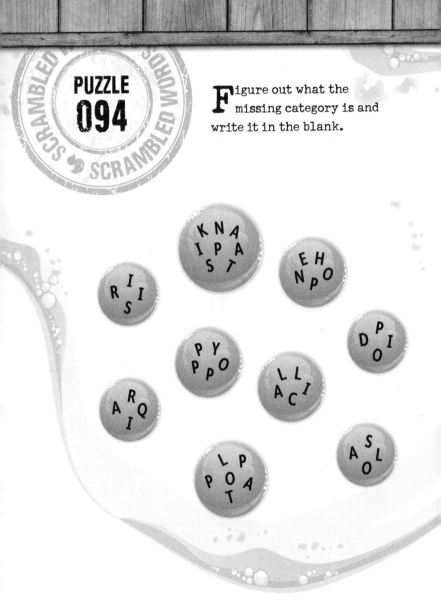

The technical term for "heart-shaped" is *cordiform*.

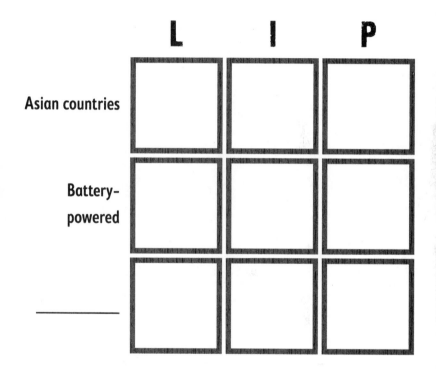

	L	I	P
Asian countries			
Battery-powered			
_____			

Answers on page 276.

Q: What does the Scoville heat index measure? A: The spiciness of food.

Figure out what the missing category is and write it in the blank.

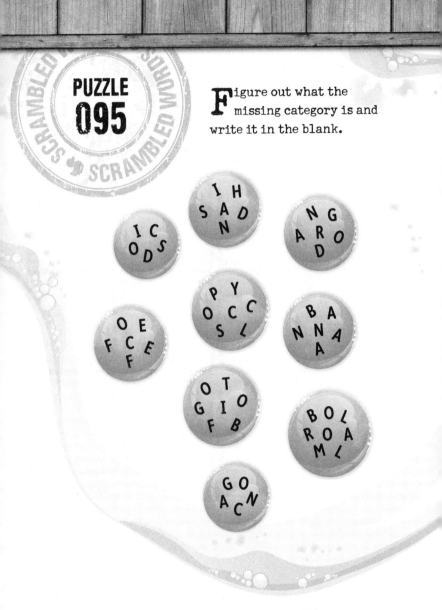

While at Harvard, former vice president Al Gore...

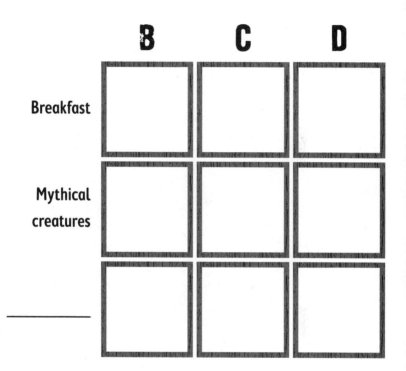

	B	C	D
Breakfast			
Mythical creatures			
_____			

Answers on page 276.

...lived in the same dorm as actor Tommy Lee Jones.

PUZZLE 096

Figure out what the missing category is and write it in the blank.

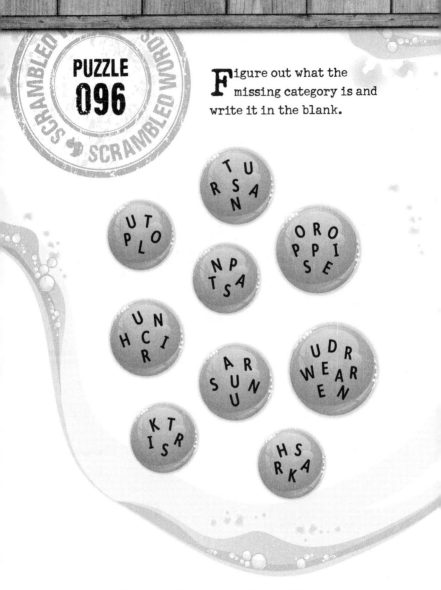

T U S A N R

U T P L O

O R O P P I S E

N P T S A

U N H C I R

A R S U N U

U D R W E A R E N

K T R I S

H S R K A

Only state without a national park: Delaware.

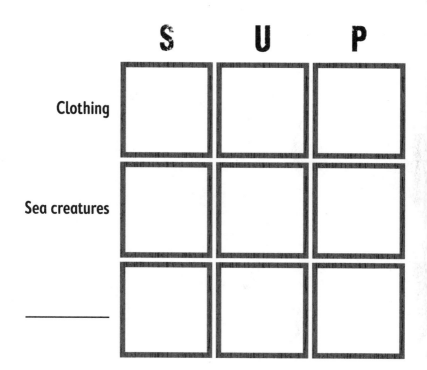

	S	**U**	**P**
Clothing			
Sea creatures			
_____			

Answers on page 277.

Herring communicate by passing gas.

Figure out what the missing category is and write it in the blank.

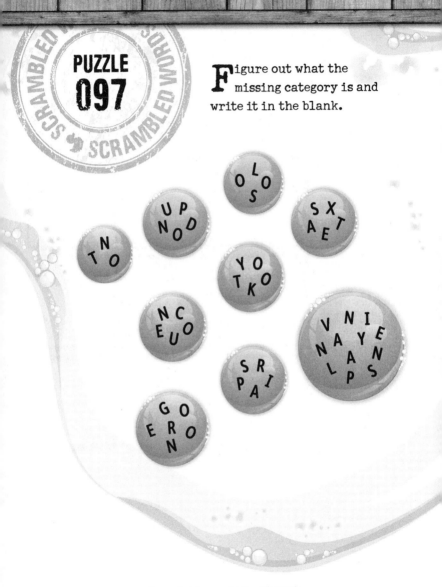

Some babies are born with teeth.

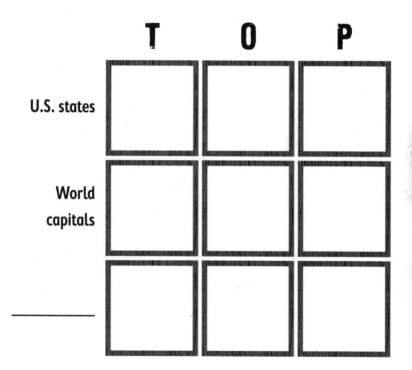

	T	**O**	**P**
U.S. states			
World capitals			
_____			

Answers on page 277.

Number of golf balls left on the moon by *Apollo* astronauts: two.

Figure out what the missing category is and write it in the blank.

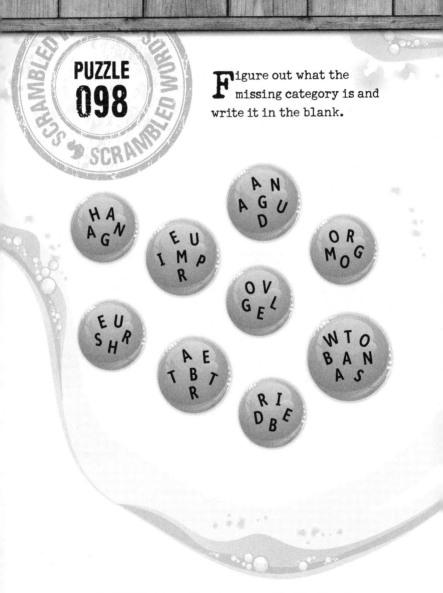

A
N
A G U
D

H A
A G N

E U
I M P
R

O R
M O G

O V
G E L

E U
S H R

W T O
B A N
A S

A E
T B T
R

R I E
D B

The NFL's Baltimore Ravens are named for "The Raven"…

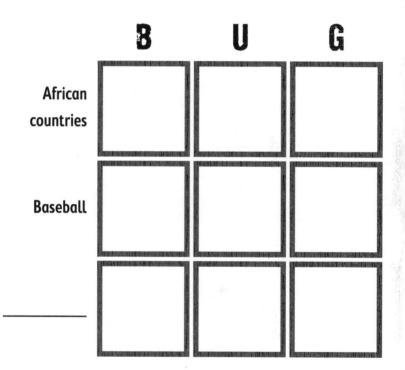

	B	**U**	**G**
African countries			
Baseball			
_____			

Answers on page 277.

...a poem by onetime Baltimore resident Edgar Allan Poe.

Figure out what the missing category is and write it in the blank.

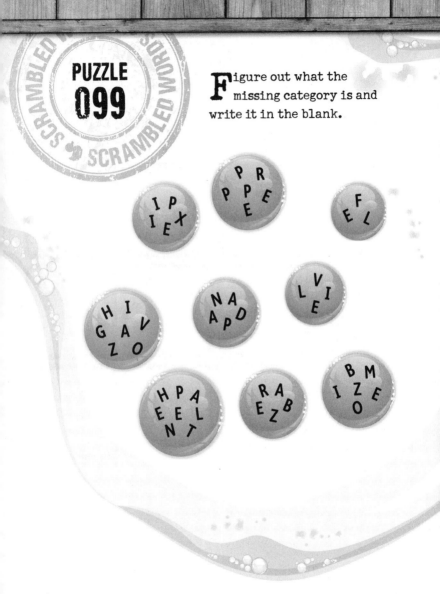

IPIEX

PRPPEE

EFL

HIGAVZO

NAAPD

LVIE

HPAEELNT

RAEZB

BMIZEO

Naperville Central High School in Illinois is the only...

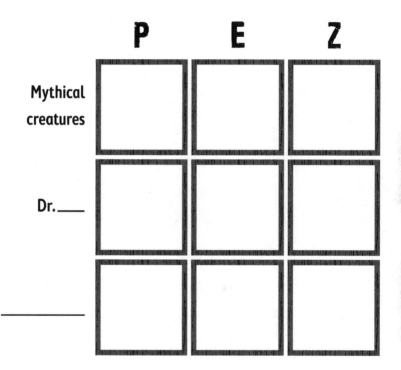

	P	**E**	**Z**
Mythical creatures			
Dr.___			
_____			

Answers on page 277.

...high school in the U.S. with its own Egyptian mummy.

Figure out what the missing category is and write it in the blank.

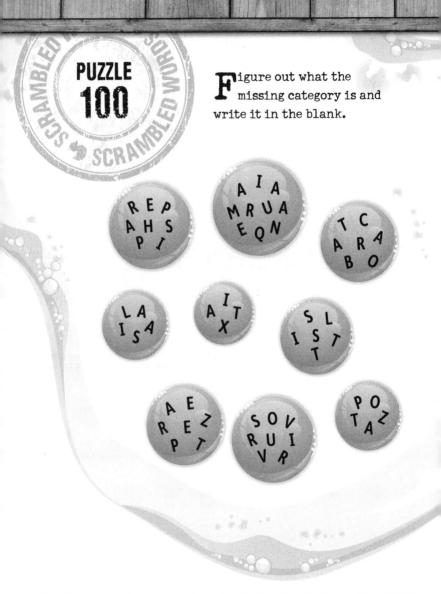

REPAHSPI

AIAMRUAEQN

TCARABO

LAISA

AITX

SLISTT

AEREZPT

SOVRUIVR

POZTA

First American hockey team to win the Stanley Cup: Seattle Metropolitans (1917).

	S	**A**	**T**
At the circus			
TV shows			
_____			

Answers on page 277.

Technically, green peppers, zucchini, cucumbers, and tomatoes are all fruits.

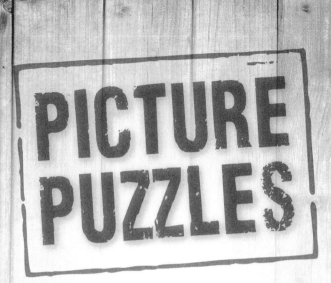

PICTURE PUZZLES

I n this section, we've substituted the scrambled letters of one of the words with a picture of an object. Once you figure out what the object is, unscramble the letters of its name and put that word in the correct square. Let's say you've got a picture of a coat, for example, and one of the categories is "Mexican food." All you have to do is scramble the letters of COAT to get TACO. Then write that in the square under the letter T.

CRAMBLED WO

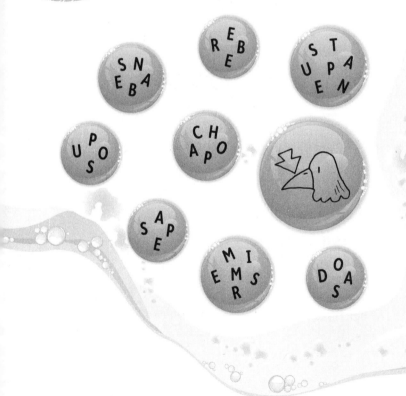

Figure out the name of the object that's pictured in the circle and unscramble the letters to get another word that fits into one of the squares.

R E B E

S N A E B

S T U P A E N

U P O S

C H A P O

S A P E

M I E M R S

D O A S

Gangster Al Capone sponsored Chicago soup kitchens during the Great Depression.

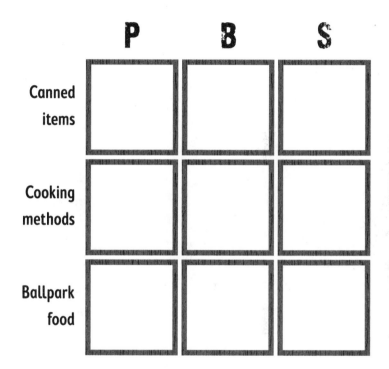

	P	**B**	**S**
Canned items			
Cooking methods			
Ballpark food			

Answers on page 278.

The unique taste of NYC pizza has been attributed to the city's water.

PUZZLE 102

SCRAMBLED WORDS

Figure out the name of the object that's pictured in the circle and unscramble the letters to get another word that fits into one of the squares.

L A R E

R E I D N

K E U D

T R Y A E E

R R R E O

C H T R C A

T U O C N

B O E D U L

If you could drive a car at 60 mph into space it would…

210

D E C

	D	E	C
"Restaurant" synonyms			
Playing baseball			
Royal titles			

Answers on page 278.

...take 6 months to reach the moon.

Figure out the name of the object that's pictured in the circle and unscramble the letters to get another word that fits into one of the squares.

3rd Month

T A E L M U

M A A D

I N A C

N A N C O

S O N S S A M

L A R A M

L E P S L

R E N S I

Q: What function do your arrector pili muscles perform? A: They cause goose bumps.

	S	**A**	**C**
Bible characters			
Making magic			
Loud things			

Answers on page 278.

First NBA player to break a backboard: Chuck Connors.

Figure out the name of the object that's pictured in the circle and unscramble the letters to get another word that fits into one of the squares.

S A
E S H

N I
E C H
Y M

F R
T E
A

T
A R
V A
A

K N
A
H T

S N
T G O

G L I
H I T
W T

J O
C U

U.S. president Woodrow Wilson's actual first name was Thomas.

	C	**A**	**T**
Before "you"			
Movie titles			
Fireplace things			

Answers on page 278.

You can make toothpaste out of dried cuttlefish bones.

Figure out the name of the object that's pictured in the circle and unscramble the letters to get another word that fits into one of the squares.

My Thoughts

C A
E H P

C R
P H O

Z E
F N R
O

E F
E
R

E F E
N C

W I R
D A E
V Y

R E
N N D
I

D O C
U R E
P

In the 1970s, Hostess sold grape-, orange-, and cherry-flavored potato chips.

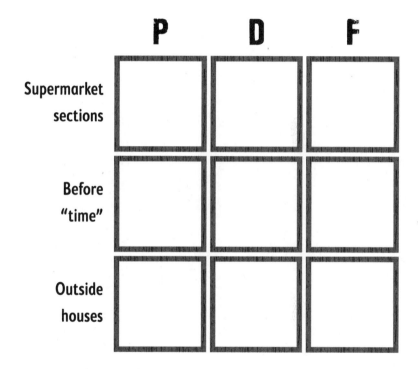

	P	**D**	**F**
Supermarket sections			
Before "time"			
Outside houses			

Answers on page 278.

First movie filmed in color to win the Best Picture Oscar: *Gone With the Wind* (1939).

Figure out the name of the object that's pictured in the circle and unscramble the letters to get another word that fits into one of the squares.

L Y I K M

U L L Y F

T O O F

L E I M

T E L I N

C E F A R N

L A C I N E D

G O O L I N M A

The longest filibuster speech in the U.S. Senate lasted 24 hours, 18 minutes. It was...

	I	M	F
Measuring units			
Countries			
"L" in the middle			

Answers on page 279.

...delivered in 1957 by Strom Thurmond, opposing the Civil Rights Acts (which passed).

Figure out the name of the object that's pictured in the circle and unscramble the letters to get another word that fits into one of the squares.

T E U L

J O A B N

D I N A E M

M A A B I R

R O D L

R A O M Y

D R B N A

P I B O S H

In 2012, Switzerland unveiled the world's first solar-powered ski lift.

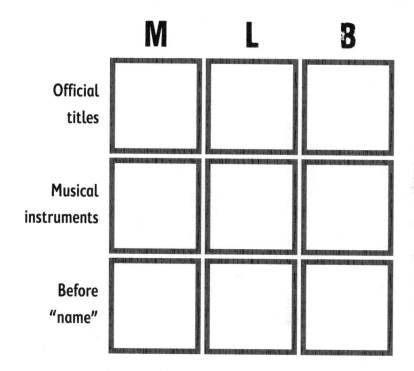

	M	L	B
Official titles			
Musical instruments			
Before "name"			

Answers on page 279.

Q: Who is Stefani Joanne Angelina Germanotta? A: Lady Gaga.

Figure out the name of the object that's pictured in the circle and unscramble the letters to get another word that fits into one of the squares.

DEEDE

WOODGODD

DIYCN

TPLAACA

DALIN

DEILNN

ANDNO

NOCCRTAT

First TV show to use closed-captioning: PBS' *The French Chef* (1972).

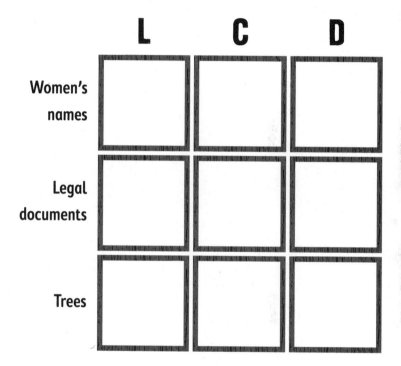

	L	C	D
Women's names			
Legal documents			
Trees			

Answers on page 279.

Shortest U.S. president: James Madison (5'4"). Tallest: Abraham Lincoln (6'4").

Figure out the name of the object that's pictured in the circle and unscramble the letters to get another word that fits into one of the squares.

T R S A

C H T M A

M I O C C

K A S U E Q

C H S T E K

K L C A H

T O E C M

K S L L U O M

Animals that prefer twilight are called *crespuscular*.

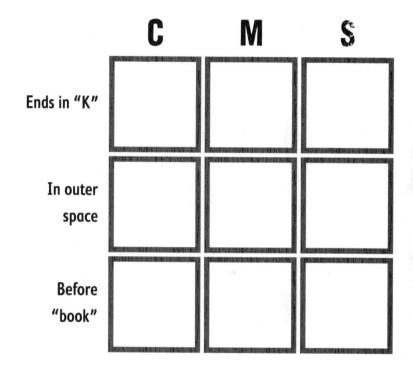

	C	**M**	**S**
Ends in "K"			
In outer space			
Before "book"			

Answers on page 279.

Crickets' ears are located just below the "knees" on their front legs.

SCRAMBLED WORDS

Figure out the name of the object that's pictured in the circle and unscramble the letters to get another word that fits into one of the squares.

E L G

R L Y A R

C R O S A

D N O P

T R P E E

E V R O

G O L O N A

C P T A H

In 1986, Ted Nugent offered to buy the Muzak company for $10 million...

	L	**O**	**P**
Bodies of water			
Men's names			
Before "work"			

Answers on page 279.

...so that he could shut it down. His bid was rejected.

Figure out the name of the object that's pictured in the circle and unscramble the letters to get another word that fits into one of the squares.

V I L
O E

F I T
O L D
U E

P C F
I A
A C

C R I
B H

C L
I T A
B

U T N
B

C H I
R E
P T

T R A
I N L
E O

A 2012 poll revealed that 2% of voters thought Mitt Romney's first name was Mittens.

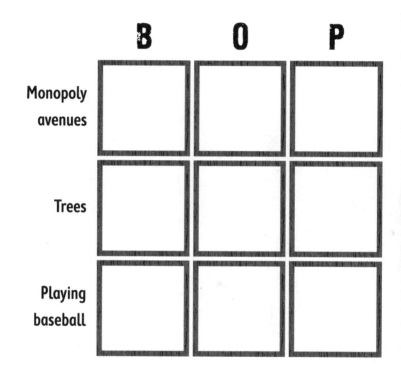

	B	**O**	**P**
Monopoly avenues			
Trees			
Playing baseball			

Answers on page 280.

The arteries of a blue whale's heart are so big that a human could crawl through them.

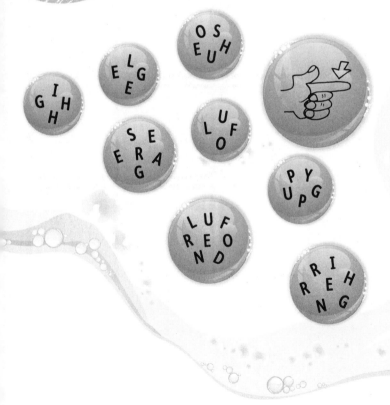

Figure out the name of the object that's pictured in the circle and unscramble the letters to get another word that fits into one of the squares.

O S E U H

E L G E

G I H H

L U F O

S E E R A G

P Y U P G

L U F R E O N D

R I R E H N G

The phrase "always a bridesmaid, never a bride" originated in…

	F	**G**	**H**
TV shows			
Before "ball"			
Fish			

Answers on page 280.

...the 1920s in commercials for Listerine mouthwash.

PUZZLE 113

Figure out the name of the object that's pictured in the circle and unscramble the letters to get another word that fits into one of the squares.

R U S
R T R E
E A

R O V
R O E
N G

F E
O F
T E

F E L
S

S T R E
N
O A

K R
S C E
U

S M E
G A

I M E
T

The only countries that haven't adopted the metric system: Myanmar, Liberia, and the U.S.

	S	**G**	**T**
Magazines			
Sweet treats			
Elected officials			

Answers on page 280.

In 2005, the cardboard box was inducted into the Toy Hall of Fame.

Figure out the name of the object that's pictured in the circle and unscramble the letters to get another word that fits into one of the squares.

G I R N

D U O N R

S N E R V A

C O S R B N

L U L B

L E L B

A R E I D R S

R S O O T R E

Studies show: Ants have graveyards.

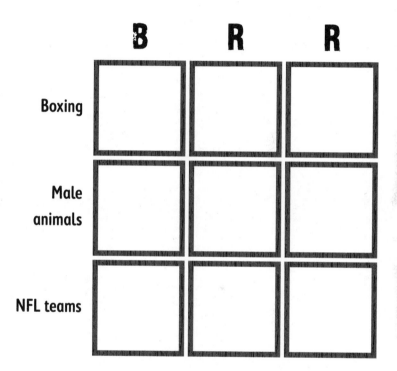

	B	**R**	**R**
Boxing			
Male animals			
NFL teams			

Answers on page 280.

Explorer I, the first satellite launched by the U.S., weighed just 31 pounds.

Figure out the name of the object that's pictured in the circle and unscramble the letters to get another word that fits into one of the squares.

K O
E p R

O K E
B R
O D

L A
E B C

O C
P E L
I

S P
C A R

L O R
E T E
U T

C O M P
O N I T
A L O S

L O
E P P
E

Before writing *The Lord of the Rings*, J. R. R. Tolkien worked...

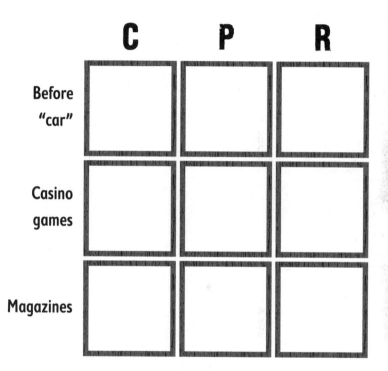

	C	**P**	**R**
Before "car"			
Casino games			
Magazines			

Answers on page 280.

...as an editor for the *Oxford English Dictionary*.

Figure out the name of the object that's pictured in the circle and unscramble the letters to get another word that fits into one of the squares.

O C O C R A N

K N G A I T A S T

O L U S

S U E L B

I W N G R O

A V B E E R

L W I O N G B

S L I U E Q R R

Paul McCartney performed on the Steve Miller Band album...

	B	**R**	**S**
Music styles			
Animals			
Sports			

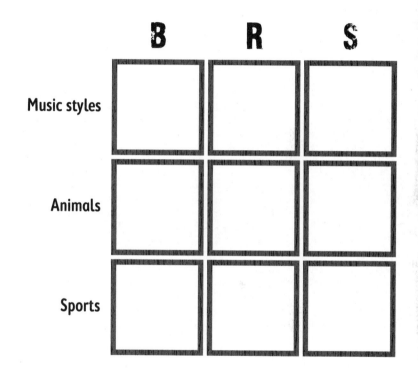

Answers on page 281.

...*Brave New World*. He was billed as Paul Ramon.

Figure out the name of the object that's pictured in the circle and unscramble the letters to get another word that fits into one of the squares.

C E I P S S

O E R K P

O T A B U

R A T T I U A I G S S

A G R R O P M

Q U I U A S R A

G E S T A

L E I S A

ABBA is an acronym of the band members' names: Agnetha, Bjorn, Benny, and Anni-frid.

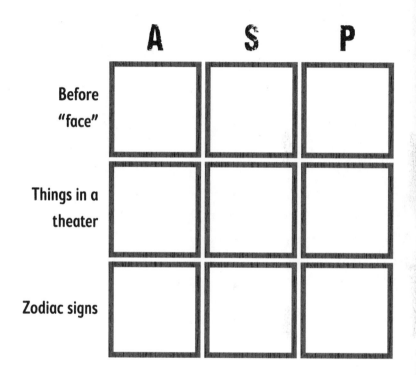

	A	S	P
Before "face"			
Things in a theater			
Zodiac signs			

Answers on page 281.

Denver was offered the 1976 Winter Olympics, but city voters declined.

PUZZLE 118

SCRAMBLED WORDS

Figure out the name of the object that's pictured in the circle and unscramble the letters to get another word that fits into one of the squares.

Johnny Carson's first guest as host of *The Tonight Show*: Groucho Marx...

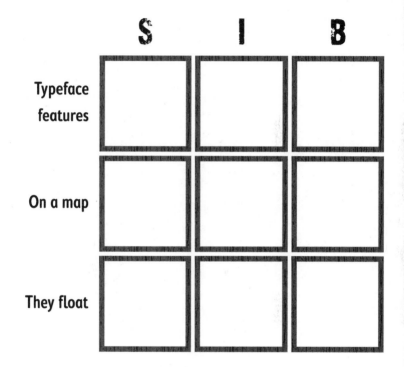

	S	**I**	**B**
Typeface features			
On a map			
They float			

Answers on page 281.

...Jay Leno's first guest: Billy Crystal.

Figure out the name of the object that's pictured in the circle and unscramble the letters to get another word that fits into one of the squares.

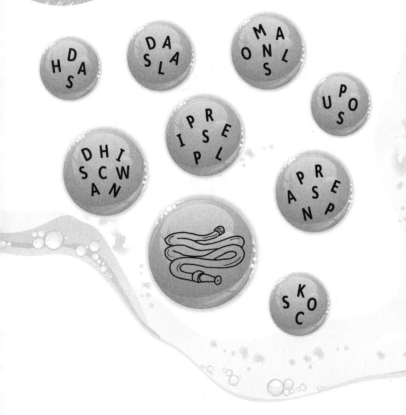

H D A S

D A S L A

M A O N L S

U P O S

I P R S E P L

D H I S C W A N

A P R S E N P

S K O C

Q. By what title did Julia Tyler, wife of U.S. president John Tyler...

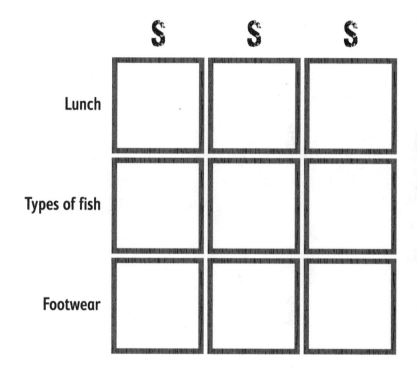

	S	S	S
Lunch			
Types of fish			
Footwear			

Answers on page 281.

...prefer to be known? A. Mrs. Presidentress.

Figure out the name of the object that's pictured in the circle and unscramble the letters to get another word that fits into one of the squares.

S I S R U E R P

E O R F

G R F O A

E R E T

H T S F A

B R E T I M

W E R O L F

I F A R T F C

Symbols used to indicate swearing in comics (such as @#$%!) are called *grawlix*.

	F	T	S
Movies			
Words that are yelled			
Growing in the yard			

Answers on page 281.

Singer Conway Twitty's real name: Harold Jenkins.

PUZZLE 121

SCRAMBLED WORDS

Figure out the name of the object that's pictured in the circle and unscramble the letters to get another word that fits into one of the squares.

T U R H

K O H O

C T H A

I D A N L D A

I S K C A Y B

M A R S C E

C H G A I N

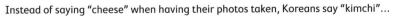

C R H O A O N

Instead of saying "cheese" when having their photos taken, Koreans say "kimchi"...

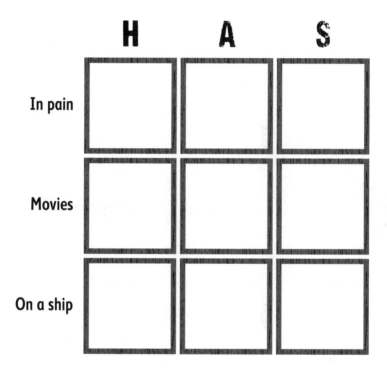

	H	A	S
In pain			
Movies			
On a ship			

Answers on page 282.

…It's a traditional Korean vegetable dish.

Figure out the name of the object that's pictured in the circle and unscramble the letters to get another word that fits into one of the squares.

P L E H

S H Y U K

T R T S T E E

D A H E

A T R E H

P T O S

A R U R H H

D U H O N

First president to throw out the first pitch at a World Series: William Taft (1910).

	S	**H**	**H**
Dogs			
Body parts			
Words that are yelled			

Answers on page 282.

Horses the size of cats roamed the forests of North America 56 million years ago.

Figure out the name of the object that's pictured in the circle and unscramble the letters to get another word that fits into one of the squares.

First NFL player to perform an end-zone dance after a touchdown: Elmo Wright (1973).

	S	W	F
Parts of a car			
Before "man"			
Animals			

Answers on page 282.

The cologne Obsession for Men has been known to attract jaguars, leopards, and tigers.

Figure out the name of the object that's pictured in the circle and unscramble the letters to get another word that fits into one of the squares.

L A T B L O

D E Y R

T R E I C D V

U C U V M A

B R L E E N D

T E E D A B

C N H E B

F E E S E D N

In 1936, Russian scientist Vladimir Lukyanov invented a computer that ran on water.

	B	**V**	**D**
Courtroom			
Election things			
Household appliances			

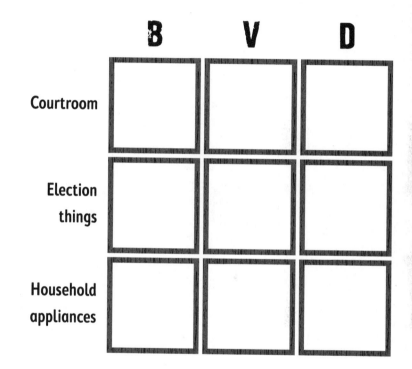

Answers on page 282.

Leo Fender—inventor of the Stratocaster guitar—couldn't play the instrument himself.

Figure out the name of the object that's pictured in the circle and unscramble the letters to get another word that fits into one of the squares.

PETEE

LEETS

DRLAIZ

DELA

LONOSA

TRTUEL

ATALIR

NATMIUTI

Kleenex was originally marketed as cold cream remover.

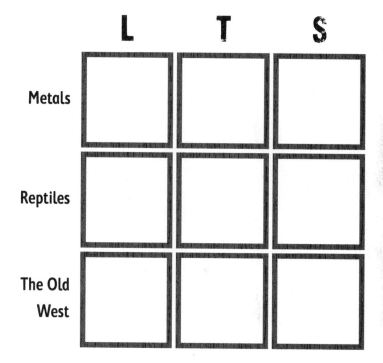

	L	T	S
Metals			
Reptiles			
The Old West			

Answers on page 282.

The act of listening to the body with a stethoscope is called *auscultation*.

ANSWERS

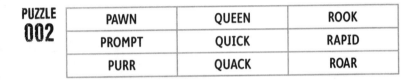

COW	BULL	STEER
CRASH	BLADE	SPEED
CARP	BASS	SOLE

PAWN	QUEEN	ROOK
PROMPT	QUICK	RAPID
PURR	QUACK	ROAR

CAR	AIRPLANE	BOAT
CLINTON	ADAMS	BUSH
CHEST	ARM	BELLY

TWO	EIGHT	NINE
TARGET	EXXON	NIKE
THOMAS	ERIC	NATHAN

DUNE	OASIS	CAMEL
DAISY	ORCHID	CROCUS
DRUM	ORGAN	CELLO

PUZZLE 006	MOOSE	ELK	DEER
	MAKE	EVEN	DROP
	MIKE	ERNIE	DAVE

PUZZLE 007	COOKIE	PIE	ROLL
	CARDINALS	PADRES	REDS
	COWBOY	POSSE	RODEO

PUZZLE 008	PEPSI	COKE	SPRITE
	POLO	CYCLING	SOCCER
	POUR	CAST	STAIRS

PUZZLE 009	KITTEN	FAWN	COLT
	KNEE	FINGER	CHIN
	KENNEDY	FORD	CARTER

PUZZLE 010	PENCIL	CRAYON	BRUSH
	PANCAKE	CEREAL	BACON
	POODLE	COLLIE	BEAGLE

ANSWERS

BLUE	INDIGO	GREEN
BELGIUM	ITALY	GREECE
BRAWL	ICING	GOALIE

INDIA	NEPAL	CHINA
IODINE	NEON	CARBON
IDAHO	NEVADA	COLORADO

BANANA	APPLE	MELON
BONO	ADELE	MADONNA
BURRO	ASS	MULE

CONGO	AMAZON	DANUBE
CAMEL	ALLIGATOR	DOG
CAROL	ALICE	DORIS

CORN	OATS	WHEAT
CEDAR	OAK	WILLOW
CALIFORNIA	OHIO	WYOMING

PUZZLE 016

GREASE	EVITA	MAME
GLOW	EFFECT	MATH
GOOSE	EAGLE	MALLARD

PUZZLE 017

LIMBO	BALLET	JIG
LEBANON	BRAZIL	JAPAN
LEG	BRAIN	JAW

PUZZLE 018

FRAME	GEAR	HANDLEBARS
FALCON	GULL	HAWK
FAIRY	GENIE	HOBBIT

PUZZLE 019

DRE	PHIL	SPOCK
DUTCH	POSTAL	STEADY
DISH	PLATE	SPOON

PUZZLE 020

CLUB	PAR	ROUGH
CLOCK	PENNY	RING
CLEVELAND	POLK	ROOSEVELT

ANSWERS

CHILE	ARGENTINA	PERU
CHISEL	AWL	PLIERS
CASHEW	ACORN	PISTACHIO

BERRIES	TEA	WAFFLE
BROWN	TAN	WHITE
BREAK	TANGO	WALTZ

LOIRE	MISSISSIPPI	NILE
LINCOLN	MONROE	NIXON
LIME	MANGO	NECTARINE

FERRY	AUTOMOBILE	TRAIN
FACE	ANKLE	TOOTH
FLORIDA	ALABAMA	TENNESSEE

LOFT	PLOW	SHEEP
LOAFER	PUMP	SANDAL
LONDON	PERTH	SEOUL

ANSWERS

PUZZLE 026

VOLGA	HUDSON	SNAKE
VOLVO	HONDA	SAAB
VALUE	HANG	SLEEP

PUZZLE 027

PUCK	RINK	SKATE
PINE	REDWOOD	SPRUCE
POWER	RACE	SENSE

PUZZLE 028

STERN	ENGINE	CABIN
STARFISH	EEL	CRAB
SWALLOW	EGRET	CHICKADEE

PUZZLE 029

SUDAN	IRAN	RWANDA
SPIDER	INK	RAVEN
STEVEN	ISAAC	RONALD

PUZZLE 030

MAJOR	PRIVATE	GENERAL
MUSTARD	PAPRIKA	GINGER
MUSKRAT	PIG	GIRAFFE

ANSWERS

PUZZLE 031

CHERRY	ORANGE	PEAR
CHEESE	ONION	PICKLE
CHEETAH	OCELOT	PANTHER

PUZZLE 032

RECTANGLE	OVAL	TRIANGLE
RALPH	OTTO	TOM
RHODES	OAHU	TAHITI

PUZZLE 033

BIBLE	ATLAS	NOVEL
BOSTON	ALBANY	NASHVILLE
BREAKFAST	ANY	NIGHT

PUZZLE 034

FLUTE	OBOE	XYLOPHONE
FEDEX	ORACLE	XEROX
FORCEPS	OPERATION	X-RAY

PUZZLE 035

KOJAK	LASSIE	MASH
KANSAS	LOUISIANA	MAINE
KANGAROO	LIZARD	MOUSE

PUZZLE 036

DECK	RUDDER	SAIL
DRACULA	RAMBO	SHREK
DOLITTLE	RUTH	SEUSS

PUZZLE 037

MONK	ROSEANNE	SEINFELD
MEXICO	RUSSIA	SWEDEN
MERCEDES	RENAULT	SUBARU

PUZZLE 038

MANX	PERSIAN	SIAMESE
MARLIN	PERCH	SARDINE
MASK	PADS	STICK

PUZZLE 039

MOROCCO	EGYPT	NIGERIA
MILK	ENCHANTED	NETWORK
MERCURY	EARTH	NEPTUNE

PUZZLE 040

PAYPAL	EBAY	GOOGLE
PEARL	EMERALD	GARNET
PRICED	ESTIMATE	GROUND

ANSWERS

NYLON	ACRYLIC	POLYESTER
NISSAN	AUDI	PORSCHE
NANCY	ANNE	PAULA

RHINE	SEINE	THAMES
RADISH	SPINACH	TURNIP
RISK	SORRY	TABOO

WAIST	ELBOW	TOE
WILSON	EISENHOWER	TAFT
WASP	EARWIG	TERMITE

VIKINGS	COWBOYS	RAMS
VIETNAM	CHAD	ROMANIA
VOLLEYBALL	CURLING	RUGBY

TELLER	INTEREST	CASH
TIN	IRON	COPPER
TRIPLE	INNING	CATCH

PUZZLE 046

JUMP	FIGHT	KICK
JACKAL	FROG	KOALA
JIVE	FOXTROT	KRUMPING

PUZZLE 047

MICROSOFT	APPLE	DELL
MOSCOW	ATHENS	DUBLIN
MUDSLIDE	AVALANCHE	DROUGHT

PUZZLE 048

SWISS	AMERICAN	NACHO
STAMP	ADDRESS	NAME
SUSAN	ANDREA	NAOMI

PUZZLE 049

POTATO	ASPARAGUS	LETTUCE
PANAMA	AUSTRIA	LIBYA
PEONY	AZALEA	LOTUS

PUZZLE 050

TURBAN	BEANIE	SOMBRERO
TENNIS	BADMINTON	SQUASH
TOPEKA	BOISE	SALEM

ANSWERS

LUNG	EYE	THIGH
LOON	EMU	TERN
LISA	ELLA	TAMMY

(extra) GNVEN

SAUSAGE	HAM	EGGS
SHIN	HAND	EAR
SHOVEL	HOE	EDGER

(extra) SPGHEI

MOO	GOBBLE	BARK
MINT	GARLIC	BASIL
MARCH	GERMY	BIRTH

(extra) MEMB

RUNNER	OPEN	DIVVY
RUBY	OPAL	DIAMOND
ROBIN	ORIOLE	DOVE

(extra) RURXE

CHAIR	UMBRELLA	TOWEL
CLOWN	UNICYCLE	TENT
CLUE	UNO	TWISTER

(extra) SMIIHU

PUZZLE
056

DONKEY	HORSE	LLAMA
DESK	HALL	LOCKER
DRILL	HAMMER	LEVEL

(extra) DRUBI

PUZZLE
057

BREAD	CUPCAKE	DOUGHNUT
BERET	CAP	DERBY
BUICK	CHRYSLER	DODGE

(extra) PAMEM

PUZZLE
058

ASTER	ROSE	TULIP
ALIEN	ROCKY	TROY
ANTELOPE	RABBIT	TOAD

(extra) BIBBE

PUZZLE
059

PEDAL	BRAKE	SPOKE
PELICAN	BOOBY	SPARROW
POKER	BET	SLOTS

(extra) GOOPR

PUZZLE
060

CHEVRON	TEXACO	SHELL
CHILI	TACO	SALSA
COW	TRACTOR	SILO

(extra) PREXLU

ANSWERS

SNICKERS	TWIX	PEZ
SPAIN	TURKEY	POLAND
SATIN	TWILL	POPLIN

(extra) SINOH

CROW	HOPI	APACHE
CYPRESS	HOLLY	ASH
CUBA	HAITI	ARUBA

(extra) CRUBL

CUE	RACK	TABLE
COOLIDGE	REAGAN	TYLER
CONCORD	RALEIGH	TRENTON

(extra) MINGOE

PAD	EASEL	CANVAS
PRINCE	ELVIS	CHER
PASS	EXPOSE	CHARGE

(extra) VUNNI

CABARET	ANNIE	WICKED
COUSIN	AUNT	WIFE
CHIMP	ARMADILLO	WOLF

(extra) CMIEP

PUZZLE 066

CHECK	DEPOSIT	SAFE
CHIVE	DILL	SAFFRON
COTTON	DENIM	SUEDE

(extra) SGPIL

PUZZLE 067

HERTZ	AVIS	DOLLAR
HONOLULU	ATLANTA	DENVER
HAWAII	ALASKA	DELAWARE

(extra) HHOMLE

PUZZLE 068

GRAPE	APRICOT	PEACH
GUITAR	ACCORDION	PIANO
GREYHOUND	AKITA	PUG

(extra) GRUOM

PUZZLE 069

MATCH	ORDER	DATE
MALI	OMAN	DENMARK
MADISON	OLYMPIA	DOVER

(extra) DREEV

PUZZLE 070

MONEY	ACCOUNT	PEN
MURDER	ASSAULT	PERJURY
MACADAMIA	ALMOND	PECAN

(extra) SSPUKL

ANSWERS

PUZZLE 071

SEAT	CHAIN	HELMET
SKIING	CRICKET	HANDBALL
SULFUR	CALCIUM	HYDROGEN

(extra) FRUMEO

PUZZLE 072

MADRID	TORONTO	VIENNA
MARIMBA	TRUMPET	VIOLIN
MAGPIE	THRUSH	VULTURE

(extra) KELOL

PUZZLE 073

SILVER	OXYGEN	NICKEL
SIOUX	OMAHA	NAVAJO
SNAKE	OTTER	NEWT

(extra) SPENTA

PUZZLE 074

ROPE	PORTHOLE	MAST
RUMBA	POLKA	MACARENA
RAG	PLAY	MEAL

(extra) GPLUET

PUZZLE 075

TRUMPET	VIOLIN	SAXOPHONE
THYME	VANILLA	SAGE
THRUSH	VEERY	SWALLOW

(extra) MROTHU

ANSWERS

PUZZLE 076

JOKER	FOUR	KING
JERRY	FRANK	KEVIN
JEEP	FIAT	KIA

The missing category is "Car makes."

PUZZLE 077

JAY	OWL	TURKEY
JUICE	OMELET	TOAST
JOHNSON	OBAMA	TRUMAN

The missing category is "U.S. presidents."

PUZZLE 078

AHOY	BRAVO	CHARGE
ANT	BEE	CRICKET
ASP	BOA	COBRA

The missing category is "Snakes."

PUZZLE 079

BOGGLE	OTHELLO	YAHTZEE
BALLAD	OPERA	YODEL
BLACK	ORANGE	YELLOW

The missing category is "Colors."

PUZZLE 080

PIGLET	FILLY	CALF
PUPPY	FOAL	CUB
PUFFIN	FINCH	CROW

The missing category is "Birds."

273

ANSWERS

FUZZ	GROUND	HAIR
FELIX	GEORGE	HOWARD
FROG	GOPHER	HYENA

The missing category is "Animals."

BUDGET	ALAMO	THRIFTY
BRAVES	ANGELS	TIGERS
BRIBERY	ARSON	THEFT

The missing category is "Crimes."

LIBERIA	MALTA	NORWAY
LIFE	MASS	NOON
LUCKY	MONEY	NEWSWEEK

The missing category is "Magazines."

BEAR	MONKEY	COYOTE
BAMBI	MULAN	CARS
BUTTER	MILK	CREAM

The missing category is "Dairy foods."

ERASE	SKETCH	PAINT
EXIT	SCREEN	POPCORN
EMINEM	STING	PINK

The missing category is "One-named singers."

ANSWERS

HUNGARY	IRELAND	PORTUGAL
HERON	IBIS	PELICAN
HOLE	IRON	PUTTER

The missing category is **"Golf."**

PUZZLE 087

MARIGOLD	VIOLET	PANSY
MALLET	VISE	PLANE
MAMBA	VIPER	PYTHON

The missing category is **"Snakes."**

PUZZLE 088

SAILOR	ADMIRAL	CAPTAIN
STAIRS	ATTIC	CLOSET
SAW	AXE	CLAMP

The missing category is **"Tools."**

PUZZLE 089

TADPOLE	LAMB	CHICK
TIGHT	LIFT	CHUCK
TOTAL	LIFE	CHEERIOS

The missing category is **"Cereal brands."**

PUZZLE 090

GOLD	URANIUM	MERCURY
GHOST	UNICORN	MERMAID
GRANDFATHER	UNCLE	MOTHER

The missing category is **"Family members."**

PUZZLE 091

CAMERA	ALARM	REMOTE
COOKING	ART	ROMANCE
CAIRO	AMSTERDAM	ROME

The missing category is **"World capitals."**

PUZZLE 092

LILY	BEGONIA	JASMINE
LOST	BONES	JEOPARDY
LACROSSE	BASEBALL	JUDO

The missing category is **"Sports."**

PUZZLE 093

MUMMY	TROLL	VAMPIRE
MIXER	TOASTER	VACUUM
MOTORCYCLE	TRUCK	VAN

The missing category is **"Transportation."**

PUZZLE 094

LAOS	IRAQ	PAKISTAN
LAPTOP	IPOD	PHONE
LILAC	IRIS	POPPY

The missing category is **"Flowers."**

PUZZLE 095

BANANA	COFFEE	DANISH
BIGFOOT	CYCLOPS	DRAGON
BALLROOM	CONGA	DISCO

The missing category is **"Dances."**

ANSWERS

SKIRT	UNDERWEAR	PANTS
SHARK	URCHIN	PORPOISE
SATURN	URANUS	PLUTO

The missing category is "Planets."
(Pluto is now classified as a dwarf planet.)

PUZZLE 097

TEXAS	OREGON	PENNSYLVANIA
TOKYO	OSLO	PARIS
TON	OUNCE	POUND

The missing category is "Weight units."

PUZZLE 098

BOTSWANA	UGANDA	GHANA
BATTER	UMPIRE	GLOVE
BRIDE	USHER	GROOM

The missing category is "People at a wedding."

PUZZLE 099

PIXIE	ELF	ZOMBIE
PEPPER	EVIL	ZHIVAGO
PANDA	ELEPHANT	ZEBRA

The missing category is "Animals."

PUZZLE 100

STILTS	ACROBAT	TRAPEZE
SURVIVOR	ALIAS	TAXI
SAPPHIRE	AQUAMARINE	TOPAZ

The missing category is "Gemstones."

PUZZLE 101

PEAS	BEANS	SOUP
POACH	BAKE	SIMMER
PEANUTS	BEER	SODA

BEAK = BAKE

PUZZLE 102

DINER	EATERY	CAFE
DOUBLE	ERROR	CATCHER
DUKE	EARL	COUNT

FACE = CAFE

PUZZLE 103

SAMSON	ADAM	CAIN
SPELL	AMULET	CHARM
SIREN	ALARM	CANNON

MARCH = CHARM

PUZZLE 104

COULD	AFTER	THANK
CUJO	AVATAR	TWILIGHT
CHIMNEY	ASHES	TONGS

CLOUD = COULD

PUZZLE 105

PRODUCE	DAIRY	FROZEN
PEACE	DINNER	FREE
PORCH	DRIVEWAY	FENCE

DIARY = DAIRY

ANSWERS

PUZZLE 106

INCH	MILE	FOOT
ICELAND	MONGOLIA	FRANCE
INLET	MILKY	FULLY

CHIN = INCH

PUZZLE 107

MAYOR	LORD	BISHOP
MARIMBA	LUTE	BANJO
MAIDEN	LAST	BRAND

SALT = LAST

PUZZLE 108

LINDA	CINDY	DONNA
LEASE	CONTRACT	DEED
LINDEN	CATALPA	DOGWOOD

EASEL = LEASE

PUZZLE 109

CHALK	MOLLUSK	SQUEAK
COMET	METEOR	STAR
COMIC	MATCH	SKETCH

REMOTE = METEOR

PUZZLE 110

LAGOON	OCEAN	POND
LARRY	OSCAR	PETER
LEG	OVER	PATCH

CANOE = OCEAN

ANSWERS

BALTIC	ORIENTAL	PACIFIC
BIRCH	OLIVE	PALM
BUNT	OUTFIELD	PITCHER

LAMP = PALM

FRINGE	GLEE	HOUSE
FOUL	GREASE	HIGH
FLOUNDER	GUPPY	HERRING

FINGER = FRINGE

SELF	GAMES	TIME
SUCKER	GUM	TOFFEE
SENATOR	GOVERNOR	TREASURER

MUG = GUM

BELL	RING	ROUND
BULL	ROOSTER	RAM
BRONCOS	RAIDERS	RAVENS

ARM = RAM

CABLE	POLICE	RENTAL
CRAPS	POKER	ROULETTE
COSMOPOLITAN	PEOPLE	REDBOOK

ANTLER = RENTAL

ANSWERS

PUZZLE 116

BLUES	ROCK	SOUL
BEAVER	RACCOON	SQUIRREL
BOWLING	ROWING	SKATING

CORK = ROCK

PUZZLE 117

ABOUT	SAVE	POKER
AISLE	STAGE	PROGRAM
AQUARIUS	SAGITTARIUS	PISCES

VASE = SAVE

PUZZLE 118

SERIF	ITALIC	BOLD
SEA	ISLAND	BORDER
SHIP	ICEBERG	BUOY

FRIES = SERIF

PUZZLE 119

SOUP	SALAD	SANDWICH
SNAPPER	SHAD	SALMON
SHOE	SOCK	SLIPPER

HOSE = SHOE

PUZZLE 120

FARGO	TRAFFIC	SHAF
FORE	TIMBER	SURP
FLOWER	TREE	SH

BRUSH = SHRUB

ANSWERS

HURT	ACHING	SORE
HOOK	ALADDIN	SCREAM
HATCH	ANCHOR	SICKBAY

ROSE = SORE

SETTER	HOUND	HUSKY
SKIN	HEAD	HEART
STOP	HURRAH	HELP

SINK = SKIN

SEAT	WINDOW	FENDER
SUPER	WOLF	FISHER
SEAL	WHALE	FERRET

PURSE = SUPER

BENCH	VERDICT	DEFENSE
BALLOT	VOTES	DEBATE
LENDER	VACUUM	DRYER

TES

	TITANIUM	STEEL
ISE	TURTLE	SERPENT
RUB	TEPEE	SALOON

281

NT